PREPARING TO CELEBRATE THE FUNERAL MASS

THROUGH DEATH TO LIFE

THIRD EDITION

JOSEPH M. CHAMPLIN

AVE MARIA PRESS · AVE · Notre Dame, Indiana

Acknowledgments:

Excerpts from the *Lectionary for Mass for Use in the Dioceses of the United States of America*, second typical edition © 2001, 1998, 1997, 1986, 1970 Confraternity of Christian Doctrine, Inc., Washington, DC. Used with permission. All rights reserved. No portion of this text may be reproduced by any means without permission in writing from the copyright owner.

Excerpts from the *Order of Christian Funerals* © 1985, International Commission on English in the Liturgy Corporation (ICEL); the English translation of some Psalm Responses from *Lectionary for Mass* © 1969, 1981, 1997, ICEL; excerpts from the English translation of *The Roman Missal* © 2010, ICEL. All rights reserved.

Texts contained in this work derived whole or in part from liturgical texts copyrighted by the International Commission on English in the Liturgy (ICEL) have been published here with the confirmation of the Committee on Divine Worship, United States Conference of Catholic Bishops. No other texts in this work have been formally reviewed or approved by the United States Conference of Catholic Bishops.

Nihil Obstat: Reverend Monsignor Michael Heintz, PhD,
                Censor librorum

Imprimatur: Most Reverend Kevin C. Rhoades,
                Bishop of Fort Wayne - South Bend
                December 6, 2011

Founded in 1865, Ave Maria Press is a Ministry of the United States Province of Holy Cross.

www.avemariapress.com

ISBN-10 1-64680-147-4

ISBN-13 978-1-64680-147-3

ebook ISBN: 978-1-64680-066-7

Cover image © Getty Images/Jupiter Images.

Cover and text design by Brian C. Conley.

Printed and bound in the United States of America.

Contents

A Message for the Family

We Christians find bright rays of hope even in the midst of our darkest times. We believe that death is not only an end, but also a beginning. Our loved one has passed from this present, temporary life to a perfect, permanent one. He or she who knew God in faith on earth now sees the Lord face-to-face in heaven. While death separates us, we will one day be reunited with all those we love in a "dwelling provided for us by God, a dwelling in the heavens, not made by hands but to last forever" (2 Corinthians 5:1).

I naturally don't know who you are or where you are. But I do understand that right now you likely feel confused, sad, stunned, or perhaps even overwhelmed by your loss. In the past you have loved others, comforted them, and shared their losses. During the hours and days just ahead it will be your turn—your time to be loved, to be comforted, and to let others help you bear the pain of your grief.

When my mother died, after a long and difficult struggle with cancer, I dreaded thoughts of the wake, Funeral Mass, burial, and luncheon afterward. Questions gnawed at me. Would I hold up? Could I keep back the tears that flowed so easily? How would I get through these public events when I really just wanted to be alone with my emptiness?

In the end, I did all of these things more or less successfully. There were some bad moments, of course, when tears came, regardless of my efforts to control them, or when words got stuck in my throat. But I was surprised by the incredible support and strength I received from family, friends, and even those I barely knew.

I truly believe you will be blessed in much the same way. The kind words and quiet presence of family members, friends, and neighbors during this profoundly difficult time will raise you from the depths of sorrow and help you carry on. I pray you are able to open your heart and receive these rich blessings.

When a Catholic dies, the Church celebrates a particular set of liturgical rites to help us through the immediate days of our grieving, to express our belief in eternal life, and to help us pray for the one who has died. These rites are organized into what is called the *Order of Christian Funerals*, which contains all the liturgical prayers, scripture readings, and blessings for use immediately following the death of a member of the Church. The *Order* provides prayers for loved ones as they gather in the presence of the body, for the wake service, funeral, final commendation (prayer of farewell), and the *Rite of Committal* (which we celebrate at the place of burial, entombment, or cremation). This booklet will help you bring order to these days of hard transition and deep sorrow by helping you take part in planning the Funeral Mass for your loved one.

Joseph M. Champlin

Using This Booklet

Through Death to Life contains the prayers, blessings, and scripture readings available to you as you help plan the Funeral Mass. Your pastor or his delegate will guide you in using this booklet to choose prayers and readings and to make decisions about a few other parts of the funeral. Once you have made your choices, you can record them on the selection sheet at the end of the booklet, and then pass it along to the priest or other pastoral minister so that your parish staff can make final preparations for the liturgy.

The funeral is the central service within the *Order of Christian Funerals* and should be a source of great comfort to all who gather for it. Planning it alongside your parish priest or his delegate can help you better express your love for the one who has died, your own profound sorrow, and your faith in our kind and merciful God who promises us eternal life.

Look first at the brief overview that begins on page viii, then read through the various prayers, scripture readings, and other options available, selecting the one from each part of the liturgy that you want to use. There are many options for the funeral for you to choose from, and you may find that you simply don't have the presence of mind or a desire to read and reflect on all of these. If that is the case, talk with your parish priest or other parish minister about how you can simplify the task.

Music is an essential part of all liturgical celebration and is especially important to the funeral. It can offer great comfort and express profound faith. This booklet does not offer musical choices because these vary greatly according to local guidelines and practices and are dependent upon parish capacities. Please speak with your pastor or his delegate about what music is available to you.

Some individuals use *Through Death to Life* to plan their own funerals. When an individual has reached a certain degree of acceptance about his or her time left in this life, reading through these pages with family and friends can be quite beautiful. This act of advance planning deepens faith, strengthens hope, and gives profound expression to the love they share. Planning one's own Funeral Mass can no doubt be a difficult experience, and yet many find that it is also deeply rewarding spiritually and emotionally. Again, this booklet can serve as a trusted companion in the process.

Overview of a Catholic Funeral

1. Introductory Rites

A Catholic funeral begins at the door of the church, where the body of the deceased is received and mourners are welcomed. The priest and assisting ministers meet the family and other loved ones at the entrance of the church, where the coffin is brought inside. The priest greets them and sprinkles the coffin with holy water, recalling the water of baptism through which the deceased entered the Church and was claimed for Christ. Family, friends, or parish representatives then drape the coffin with the pall, a white cloth that recalls the white garment in which the deceased was clothed at baptism.

The entrance procession then begins, usually accompanied by the opening hymn. Once all have reached their places a symbol of the Christian life such as a bible or a cross may be placed on the coffin, either in silence or accompanied by simple words. The presider then goes to his chair and prays aloud the Collect or opening prayer.

2. Liturgy of the Word

The *Order of Christian Funerals* calls for either one or two readings before the gospel reading. When two readings are used, it is preferable for each to be proclaimed by a different reader. A Responsorial Psalm is sung as a prayerful response to the first reading and an Alleluia or Gospel Acclamation is sung to prepare all gathered for receiving Christ present in the proclamation of the Gospel. A brief homily and the General Intercessions conclude this part of the funeral.

3. Liturgy of the Eucharist

When a funeral is celebrated outside Mass, the liturgy continues with the Final Commendation and Farewell as described in part 4.

When the Funeral Mass is celebrated, the Liturgy of the Eucharist follows. It begins with the family members or friends of the deceased bringing forward the offerings of bread and wine. The priest and assisting ministers receive the offerings and prepares them and the altar for the great Eucharistic Prayer that follows. This prayer offers to God our praise and thanksgiving by recalling what Jesus did on the night before he died while at supper with his disciples. The priest consecrates the bread and wine, which become for us the body and blood of Christ.

The Communion Rite then begins with the Lord's Prayer, which is followed by the exchange of a sign of peace and the Lamb of God. Those present who are free to receive Holy Communion then come forward to do so as an appropriate hymn is sung.

4. **Final Commendation and Farewell**
    This rite may be celebrated at the cemetery or place of committal rather than in church at the end of the funeral.

    This is often the most difficult time for mourners during the funeral liturgy, since its purpose is to help them say a final farewell and entrust their loved one to the tender mercy of our God. A member of the family or another loved one may speak briefly after communion about the one who has died. The final commendation then follows with a few words of explanation from the priest, a song of farewell that all sing together, and a prayer of commendation.

    When customary, the coffin is sprinkled with holy water and incensed. The sprinkling is another reminder of baptism in which the one who has died was claimed for eternal life and the incensation helps mourners express their profound respect for the body as a dwelling place of the Holy Spirit. A procession to the place of committal concludes the funeral liturgy. "This final procession of the funeral rite mirrors the journey of human life as a pilgrimage to God's kingdom of peace and light, the new and eternal Jerusalem" (*Order of Christian Funerals*, 148).

At times it isn't practical or possible to have a Funeral Mass, and in those instances a second form of the funeral liturgy is used. This second form has the same basic structure and contains most of the same elements as a Funeral Mass, but does not include the Liturgy of the Eucharist.

The remaining pages of *Through Death to Life* contain the options for prayers, readings, and other liturgical texts available for use in each of the four major parts of the Funeral Mass. Record your choices on the selection sheet at the end of the booklet. When you are finished, give this sheet to your parish priest or other parish minister who is helping you plan the funeral.

Watch for this symbol, which will indicate to you at what points you have a selection to make.

Introductory Rites

Greeting
Sprinkling with Holy Water
Placing of the Pall
Entrance Procession
Placing of Christian Symbols
Collect

Greeting

(OCF, 159)

The Priest, with assisting ministers, goes to the door of the church and, using one of the following formulas, or in similar words, greets those present.

A

(RM, 2)

The grace of our Lord Jesus Christ,
and the love of God,
and the communion of the Holy Spirit
be with you all.
R. And with your spirit.

B

(RM, 2)

Grace to you and peace from God our Father
and the Lord Jesus Christ.
R. And with your spirit.

C   (OCF, 69-C)

> The grace and peace of God our Father, who raised Jesus from the
> dead, be always with you.
> R. And with your spirit.

D   (OCF, 69-D)

> May the Father of mercies, the God of all consolation, be with you.
> R. And with your spirit.

Sprinkling with Holy Water   (OCF, 160 and 433)

The Priest then sprinkles the coffin with holy water, saying:

> In the waters of baptism
> N. died with Christ and rose with him to new life.
> May he (she) now share with him eternal glory.

*When the body has been cremated, the Priest sprinkles the remains with holy water,
saying:*

> As our brother/sister N. has died with the Lord,
> so may he (she) live with him in glory.

Placing of the Pall   (OCF, 161)

*[If it is the custom in the local community, the pall is then placed over the coffin by
family members, friends, or the Priest.]*

Entrance Procession   (OCF, 162)

*The Easter candle may be placed beforehand near the position the coffin will occupy
at the conclusion of the procession. The Priest and assisting ministers precede the
coffin and the mourners into the church. During the procession a psalm, song, or
responsory is sung.*

Placing of Christian Symbols (optional) (OCF 163, 86)

[A symbol of the Christian life, such as a Book of the Gospels, a bible, or a cross, may be carried in procession, then placed on the coffin, either in silence or accompanied by one of the following or similar prayers recited by the minister.]

Book of the Gospels or Bible (OCF, 400-1)

In life N. cherished the Gospel of Christ.
May Christ now greet him (her) with these words of eternal life:
Come, blessed of my Father!

Cross (OCF, 400-2)

In baptism N. received the sign of the cross.
May he (she) now share
in Christ's victory over sin and death.

Cross in Case of an Unbaptized Child (OCF, 400-3)

The cross we have brought here today was carried by the Lord
Jesus in the hour of his suffering.
We place it now on [near] this coffin as a sign of our hope for N.

As the cross is placed on (or near) the coffin, the minister says:

Lord Jesus Christ,
you loved us unto death.
Let this cross be a sign of your love for N.
and for the people you have gathered here today.

Collect (OCF, 163–64)

On reaching the altar, the Priest, with the assisting ministers, makes the customary reverence, kisses the altar, and (if incense is used) incenses it. Then he goes to the chair. When all have reached their places, the Priest invites the assembly to pray in silence for a period of time and then sings or says one of the following prayers.

Please choose one of the following prayers and record it on your selection sheet using the page number and the letter-number coding that appears as the heading of each prayer.

Outside Easter Time

B1

O God, almighty Father,
our faith professes that your Son died and rose again;
mercifully grant, that through this mystery
your servant N., who has fallen asleep in Christ,
may rejoice to rise again through him.

Who lives and reigns with you in the unity of the Holy Spirit,
one God, for ever and ever.
R. Amen.

B2

O God, whose nature
is always to forgive and to show mercy,
we humbly implore you for your servant N.,
whom you have called (this day) to journey to you,
and, since he (she) hoped and believed in you,
grant that he (she) may be led to our true homeland
to delight in its everlasting joys.

Through our Lord Jesus Christ, your Son,
who lives and reigns with you in the unity of the Holy Spirit,
one God, for ever and ever.
R. Amen.

B3

O God, who are mercy for sinners
and the happiness of your Saints,
give, we pray, to your servant N.,
for whom (today) we perform the fraternal offices of burial,
a share with your chosen ones in the blessedness you give,
so that on the day of resurrection,
freed from the bonds of mortality,
he (she) may come before your face.

Through our Lord Jesus Christ, your Son,
who lives and reigns with you in the unity of the Holy Spirit,
one God, for ever and ever.
R. Amen.

B4

O God, who have set a limit to this present life,
so as to open up an entry into eternity,
we humbly beseech you,
that by the grace of your mercy
you may command the name of your servant N.
to be inscribed in the book of life.

Through our Lord Jesus Christ, your Son,
who lives and reigns with you in the unity of the Holy Spirit,
one God, for ever and ever.
R. Amen.

During Easter Time   (RM, Funeral Mass C)

B5

Listen kindly to our prayers, O Lord:
as our faith in your Son,
raised from the dead, is deepened,
may our hope of resurrection for your departed servant N.
also find new strength.

Through our Lord Jesus Christ, your Son,
who lives and reigns with you in the unity of the Holy Spirit,
one God, for ever and ever.
R. Amen.

B6

O God, who through the ending of present things
open up the beginning of things to come,
grant, we pray, that the soul of your servant N.
may be led by you
to attain the inheritance of eternal redemption.

Through our Lord Jesus Christ, your Son,
who lives and reigns with you in the unity of the Holy Spirit,
one God, for ever and ever.
R. Amen.

General

(RM, Funeral Mass, D)

B7

O God, who alone are able to give life after death,
free your servant N. from all sins,
that he (she), who believed in the Resurrection of your Christ,
may, when the day of resurrection comes,
be united with you in glory.

Through our Lord Jesus Christ, your Son,
who lives and reigns with you in the unity of the Holy Spirit,
one God, for ever and ever.
R. Amen.

General

(OCF, 398, 1–13)

B8

God of faithfulness,
in your wisdom you have called your servant N. out of this
world;
release him (her) from the bonds of sin,
and welcome him (her) into your presence,
so that he (she) may enjoy eternal light and peace
and be raised up in glory with all your saints.

We ask this through Christ our Lord.
R. Amen.

B9

Lord, in our grief we turn to you.
Are you not the God of love
who opens your ears to all?
Listen to our prayers for your servant N.,
whom you have called out of this world:
lead him (her) to your kingdom of light and peace
and count him (her) among the saints in glory.

We ask this through Christ our Lord.
R. Amen.

B10

Holy Lord, almighty and eternal God,
hear our prayers for your servant N.,
whom you have summoned out of this world.
Forgive his (her) sins and failings
and grant him (her) a place of refreshment, light, and peace.

Let him (her) pass unharmed through the gates of death
to dwell with the blessed in light,
as you promised to Abraham and his children for ever.
Accept N. into your safekeeping
and on the great day of judgment
raise him (her) up with all the saints
to inherit your eternal kingdom.

We ask this through Christ our Lord.
R. Amen.

B11

Into your hands, O Lord,
we humbly entrust our brother/sister N.
In this life you embraced him (her) with your tender love;
deliver him (her) now from every evil
and bid him (her) enter eternal rest.

The old order has passed away:
welcome him (her) then into paradise,
where there will be no sorrow, no weeping nor pain,
but the fullness of peace and joy
with your Son and the Holy Spirit
for ever and ever.
R. Amen.

B12

Almighty God and Father,
it is our certain faith
that your Son, who died on the cross, was raised from the dead,
the firstfruits of all who have fallen asleep.
Grant that through this mystery

your servant N., who has gone to his (her) rest in Christ,
may share in the joy of his resurrection.

We ask this through our Lord Jesus Christ, your Son,
who lives and reigns with you and the Holy Spirit,
One God, for ever and ever.
R. Amen.

B13

O God,
glory of believers and life of the just,
by the death and resurrection of your Son, we are redeemed:
have mercy on your servant N.,
and make him (her) worthy to share the joys of paradise,
for he (she) believed in the resurrection of the dead.

We ask this through Christ our Lord.
R. Amen.

B14

Almighty God and Father,
by the mystery of the cross, you have made us strong;
by the sacrament of the resurrection
you have sealed us as your own.
Look kindly upon your servant N.,
now freed from the bonds of mortality,
and count him (her) among your saints in heaven.

We ask this through Christ our Lord.
R. Amen.

B15

God of loving kindness,
listen favorably to our prayers:
strengthen our belief that your Son has risen from the dead
and our hope that your servant N. will also rise again.

We ask this through our Lord Jesus Christ, your Son,
who lives and reigns with you and the Holy Spirit,
one God, for ever and ever.
R. Amen.

B16

To you, O God, the dead do not die,
and in death our life is changed, not ended.
Hear our prayers
and command the soul of your servant N.
to dwell with Abraham, your friend,
and be raised at last on the great day of judgment.
In your mercy cleanse him (her) of any sin
which he (she) may have committed through human frailty.

We ask this through Christ our Lord.
R. Amen.

B17

Lord God, in whom all find refuge,
we appeal to your boundless mercy:
grant to the soul of your servant N.
a kindly welcome,
cleansing of sin,
release from the chains of death,
and entry into everlasting life.

We ask this through Christ our Lord.
R. Amen.

B18

God of all consolation,
open our hearts to your word,
so that, listening to it, we may comfort one another,
finding light in time of darkness
and faith in time of doubt.

We ask this through Christ our Lord.
R. Amen.

B19

O God,
to whom mercy and forgiveness belong,
hear our prayers on behalf of your servant N.,
whom you have called out of this world;

and because he (she) put his (her) hope and trust in you,
command that he (she) be carried safely home to heaven
and come to enjoy your eternal reward.

We ask this through our Lord Jesus Christ, your Son,
who lives and reigns with you and the Holy Spirit,
one God, for ever and ever.
R. Amen.

B20

O God,
in whom sinners find mercy and the saints find joy,
we pray to you for our brother/sister N.,
whose body we honor with Christian burial,
that he (she) may be delivered from the bonds of death.
Admit him (her) to the joyful company of your saints
and raise him (her) on the last day
to rejoice in your presence for ever.

We ask this through our Lord Jesus Christ, your Son,
who lives and reigns with you and the Holy Spirit,
one God, for ever and ever.
R. Amen.

For a Priest   (OCF, 398,17–19)

B21

God of mercy and love,
grant to N., your servant and priest,
a glorious place at your heavenly table,
for you made him here on earth
a faithful minister of your word and sacrament.

We ask this through Christ our Lord.
R. Amen.

B22

O God,
listen favorably to our prayers
offered on behalf of your servant and priest,
and grant that N.,
who committed himself zealously to the service of your name,
may rejoice for ever in the company of your saints.

We ask this through Christ our Lord.
R. Amen.

B23

Lord God,
you chose our brother N. to serve your people as a priest
and to share the joys and burdens of their lives.
Look with mercy on him
and give him the reward of his labors,
the fullness of life promised to those who preach your holy
Gospel.

We ask this through Christ our Lord.
R. Amen.

For a Deacon   (OCF, 398, 20–21)

B24

God of mercy,
as once you chose seven men of honest repute
to serve your Church,
so also you chose N. as your servant and deacon.
Grant that he may rejoice in your eternal fellowship
with all the heralds of your Gospel,
for he was untiring in his ministry here on earth.

We ask this through Christ our Lord.
R. Amen.

B25

Lord God,
you sent your Son into the world
to preach the Good News of salvation
and to pour out his Spirit of grace upon your Church.
Look with kindness on your servant N.
As a deacon in the Church
he was strengthened by the gift of the Spirit
to preach the Good News,
to minister in your assembly,
and to do the works of charity.
Give him the reward promised
to those who show their love of you
by service to their neighbor.

We ask this through Christ our Lord.
R. Amen.

For a Religious   (OCF, 398, 22–23)

B26

All-powerful God,
we pray for our brother/sister N.,
who responded to the call of Christ
and pursued wholeheartedly the ways of perfect love.
Grant that he (she) may rejoice
on that day when your glory will be revealed
and in company with all his (her) brothers and sisters
share for ever the happiness of your kingdom.

We ask this through Christ our Lord.
R. Amen.

B27

God of blessings,
source of all holiness,
the voice of your Spirit has drawn countless men and women
to follow Jesus Christ
and to bind themselves to you
with ready will and loving heart.

Look with mercy on N.
who sought to fulfill his (her) vows to you,
and grant him (her) the reward promised to all good and
faithful servants.
May he (she) rejoice in the company of the saints
and with them praise you for ever.

We ask this through Christ our Lord.
R. Amen.

For One Who Worked in the Service of the Gospel

(OCF, 398, 24)

B28

Faithful God,
we humbly ask your mercy for your servant N.,
who worked so generously to spread the Good News:
grant him (her) the reward of his (her) labors
and bring him (her) safely to your promised land.

We ask this through Christ our Lord.
R. Amen.

For a Baptized Child

(RM, Funeral Mass E)

B29

Most compassionate God,
who in the counsels of your wisdom
have called this little child to yourself
on the very threshold of life,
listen kindly to our prayers
and grant that one day we may inherit eternal life with him (her),
whom, by the grace of Baptism, you have adopted as your
own child and who we believe is dwelling even now in your
   Kingdom.

Through our Lord Jesus Christ, your Son,
who lives and reigns with you in the unity of the Holy Spirit,
one God, for ever and ever.
R. Amen.

B30

O God, who know that our hearts
are weighed down by grief
at the death of this young child,
grant that, while we weep for him (her),
who at your bidding has departed this life so soon,
we may have faith that he (she) has gained
an eternal home in heaven.

Through our Lord Jesus Christ, your Son,
who lives and reigns with you in the unity of the Holy Spirit,
one God, for ever and ever.
R. Amen.

For a Child Who Died before Baptism   (RM, Funeral Mass F)

B31

Receive the prayers of your faithful, Lord,
and grant that those you allow to be weighed down
by their longing for the child taken from them
may be raised up by faith to hope in your compassion.

Through our Lord Jesus Christ, your Son,
who lives and reigns with you in the unity of the Holy Spirit,
one God, for ever and ever.
R. Amen.

B32

O God, searcher of hearts and most loving consoler,
who know the faith of these parents,
grant that, as they mourn their child,
now departed from this life,
they may be assured
that he (she) has been entrusted to your divine compassion.

Through our Lord Jesus Christ, your Son,
who lives and reigns with you in the unity of the Holy Spirit,
one God, for ever and ever.
R. Amen.

For a Young Person (OCF, 398-27, 28)

B33

Lord,
your wisdom governs the length of our days.
We mourn the loss of N.,
whose life has passed so quickly,
and we entrust him (her) to your mercy.
Welcome him (her) into your heavenly home
and grant him (her) the happiness of everlasting youth.

We ask this through Christ our Lord.
R. Amen.

B34

Lord God,
source and destiny of our lives,
in your loving providence
you gave us N.
to grow in wisdom, age, and grace.
Now you have called him (her) to yourself.
As we grieve the loss of one so young,
we seek to understand your purpose.
Draw him (her) to yourself
and give him (her) full stature in Christ.
May he (she) stand with all the angels and saints,
who know your love and praise your saving will.

We ask this through Christ our Lord.
R. Amen.

For Parents   (OCF, 398-29)

B35

Lord God, who commanded us to honor father and mother,
look kindly upon your servants N. and N.,
have mercy upon them
and let us see them again in eternal light.

We ask this through Christ our Lord.
R. Amen.

For a Parent   (OCF, 398, 30)

B36

God of our ancestors in faith,
by the covenant made on Mount Sinai
you taught your people to strengthen the bonds of family
through faith, honor, and love.
Look kindly upon N.,
a father/mother who sought to bind his (her) children to you.
Bring him (her) one day to our heavenly home
where the saints dwell in blessedness and peace.

We ask this through Christ our Lord.
R. Amen.

For a Married Couple   (OCF, 398, 31–33)

B37

Lord God,
whose covenant is everlasting,
have mercy upon the sins of your servants N. and N.;
as their love for each other united them on earth,
so let your love join them together in heaven.

We ask this through Christ our Lord.
R. Amen.

B38

Eternal Father,
in the beginning you established the love of man and woman
as a sign of creation.
Your own Son loves the Church as a spouse.
Grant mercy and peace to N. and N. who,
by their love for each other,
were signs of the creative love
which binds the Church to Christ.

We ask this in the name of Jesus our Lord.
R. Amen.

B39

Lord God,
giver of all that is true and lovely and gracious,
you created in marriage a sign of your covenant.
Look with mercy upon N. and N.
You blessed them in their companionship,
and in their joys and sorrows you bound them together.
Lead them into eternal peace,
and bring them to the table
where the saints feast together in your heavenly home.

We ask this through Christ our Lord.
R. Amen.

For a Wife (OCF, 398, 34)

B40

Eternal God,
you made the union of man and woman
a sign of the bond between Christ and the Church.
Grant mercy and peace to N.,
who was united in love with her husband.
May the care and devotion of her life on earth
find a lasting reward in heaven.
Look kindly on her husband and family/children

as now they turn to your compassion and love.
Strengthen their faith and lighten their loss.

We ask this through Christ our Lord.
R. Amen.

For a Husband   (OCF, 398, 35)

B41

Eternal God,
you made the union of man and woman
a sign of the bond between Christ and the Church.
Grant mercy and peace to N.,
who was united in love with his wife.
May the care and devotion of his life on earth
find a lasting reward in heaven.
Look kindly on his wife and family/children
as now they turn to your compassion and love.
Strengthen their faith and lighten their loss.

We ask this through Christ our Lord.
R. Amen.

For a Non-Christian Married to a Catholic   (OCF, 398, 36)

B42

Almighty and faithful Creator,
all things are of your making,
all people are shaped in your image.
We now entrust the soul of N. to your goodness.
In your infinite wisdom and power,
work in him (her) your merciful purpose,
known to you alone from the beginning of time.
Console the hearts of those who love him (her)
in the hope that all who trust in you
will find peace and rest in your kingdom.

We ask this in the name of Jesus the Lord.
R. Amen.

For an Elderly Person (OCF, 398, 37–38)

B43

God of endless ages,
from one generation to the next
you have been our refuge and strength.
Before the mountains were born
or the earth came to be,
you are God.
Have mercy now on your servant N.
whose long life was spent in your service.
Give him (her) a place in your kingdom,
where hope is firm for all who love
and rest is sure for all who serve.

We ask this through Christ our Lord.
R. Amen.

B44

God of mercy,
look kindly on your servant N.
who has set down the burden of his (her) years.
As he (she) served you faithfully throughout his (her) life,
may you give him (her) the fullness of your peace and joy.
We give thanks for the long life of N.,
now caught up in your eternal love.

We make our prayer in the name of Jesus who is our risen
Lord now and for ever.
R. Amen.

For One Who Died after a Long Illness (OCF, 398, 39–41)

B45

God of deliverance,
you called our brother/sister N.
to serve you in weakness and pain,
and gave him (her) the grace of sharing the cross of your Son.

Reward his (her) patience and forbearance,
and grant him (her) the fullness of Christ's victory.

We ask this through Christ our Lord.
R. Amen.

B46

Most faithful God,
lively is the courage of those who hope in you.
Your servant N. suffered greatly
but placed his (her) trust in your mercy.
Confident that the petition of those who mourn
pierces the clouds and finds an answer,
we beg you, give rest to N.
Do not remember his (her) sins
but look upon his (her) sufferings
and grant him (her) refreshment, light, and peace.

We ask this through Christ our Lord.
R. Amen.

B47

O God,
you are water for our thirst
and manna in our desert.
We praise you for the life of N.
and bless your mercy
that has brought his (her) suffering to an end.
Now we beg that same endless mercy
to raise him (her) to new life.
Nourished by the food and drink of heaven,
may he (she) rest for ever
in the joy of Christ our Lord.
R. Amen.

For One Who Died Suddenly   (OCF, 398, 42)

B48

Lord,
as we mourn the sudden death of our brother/sister,
show us the immense power of your goodness
and strengthen our belief
that N. has entered into your presence.

We ask this through Christ our Lord.
R. Amen.

For One Who Died Accidentally or Violently   (OCF, 398, 43)

B49

Lord our God,
you are always faithful and quick to show mercy.
Our brother/sister N.
was suddenly [and violently] taken from us.
Come swiftly to his (her) aid,
have mercy on him (her),
and comfort his (her) family and friends
by the power and protection of the cross.

We ask this through Christ our Lord.
R. Amen.

For One Who Died by Suicide   (OCF, 398, 44–45)

B50

God, lover of souls,
you hold dear what you have made
and spare all things, for they are yours.
Look gently on your servant N.,
and by the blood of the cross
forgive his (her) sins and failings.

Remember the faith of those who mourn
and satisfy their longing for that day
when all will be made new again
in Christ, our risen Lord,
who lives and reigns with you for ever and ever.
R. Amen.

B51

Almighty God and Father of all,
you strengthen us by the mystery of the cross
and with the sacrament of your Son's resurrection.
Have mercy on our brother/sister N.
Forgive all his (her) sins and grant him (her) peace.
May we who mourn this sudden death be comforted
and consoled by your power and protection.

We ask this through Christ our Lord.
R. Amen.

For Several Persons   (OCF, 398-46, 47)

B52

O Lord,
you gave new life to N. and N.
in the waters of baptism;
show mercy to them now,
and bring them to the happiness of life in your kingdom.

We ask this through Christ our Lord.
R. Amen.

B53

All-powerful God,
whose mercy is never withheld
from those who call upon you in hope,
look kindly on your servants N. and N.,
who departed this life confessing your name,
and number them among your saints for evermore.

We ask this through Christ our Lord.
R. Amen.

Liturgy of the Word

About the Readings
First Reading
Outside Easter Time: Old Testament
During Easter Time: New Testament
Responsorial Psalm
Second Reading
Alleluia Verse and Verse before the Gospel
Gospel Reading
General Intercessions

About the Readings

In collaboration with the Priest or other parish minister assisting you, select one each from the choices for first reading, responsorial psalm, second reading, alleluia verse, and gospel reading. Choices can be recorded on the selection sheet using the letter-number coding that appears on the left side of the heading for each reading. Please also record the page number. The number on the right in parentheses is the lectionary number for that reading. It will be used by parish personnel to mark the lectionary for whoever will read during the Funeral Mass.

*When the situation warrants, a single reading may be chosen for use before the gospel.
**Non-biblical texts may not replace scriptural readings at the Funeral Mass.

First Reading

Outside Easter Time: Old Testament

C1   He acted in an excellent and noble way as he had the resurrection of the dead in view.

2 Maccabees 12:43–46
(1011-1)

A reading from the second Book of Maccabees

> Judas, the ruler of Israel,
> > took up a collection among all his soldiers,
> > amounting to two thousand silver drachmas,
> > which he sent to Jerusalem to provide for an expiatory sacrifice.
> In doing this he acted in a very excellent and noble way,
> > inasmuch as he had the resurrection of the dead in view;
> > for if he were not expecting the fallen to rise again,
> > it would have been useless and foolish to pray for them in death.
> But if he did this with a view to the splendid reward
> > that awaits those who had gone to rest in godliness,
> > it was a holy and pious thought.
> Thus he made atonement for the dead
> > that they might be freed from this sin.

The word of the Lord.

C2   I know that my Vindicator lives.

Job 19:1, 23–27a
(1011-2)

A reading from the Book of Job

> Job answered Bildad the Shuhite and said:
> Oh, would that my words were written down!
> > Would that they were inscribed in a record:
> That with an iron chisel and with lead
> > they were cut in the rock forever!

But as for me, I know that my Vindicator lives,
    and that he will at last stand forth upon the dust;
Whom I myself shall see:
    my own eyes, not another's, shall behold him;
And from my flesh I shall see God;
    my inmost being is consumed with longing.

The word of the Lord.

C3 As sacrificial offerings he took them to himself.

Long version: Wisdom 3:1–9
(1011-3)

A reading from the Book of Wisdom

The souls of the just are in the hand of God,
    and no torment shall touch them.
They seemed, in the view of the foolish, to be dead;
    and their passing away was thought an affliction
    and their going forth from us, utter destruction.
But they are in peace.
For if before men, indeed, they be punished,
    yet is their hope full of immortality;
Chastised a little, they shall be greatly blessed,
    because God tried them
    and found them worthy of himself.
As gold in the furnace, he proved them,
    and as sacrificial offerings he took them to himself.
In the time of their visitation they shall shine,
    and shall dart about as sparks through stubble;
They shall judge nations and rule over peoples,
    and the Lord shall be their King forever.
Those who trust in him shall understand truth,
    and the faithful shall abide with him in love:
Because grace and mercy are with his holy ones,
    and his care is with his elect.

The word of the Lord.

C3

Short version: Wisdom 3:1–6, 9

A reading from the Book of Wisdom

> The souls of the just are in the hand of God
> > and no torment shall touch them.
> They seemed, in the view of the foolish, to be dead;
> > and their passing away was thought an affliction
> > and their going forth from us, utter destruction.
> But they are in peace.
> For if in the eyes of men, indeed, they be punished,
> > yet is their hope full of immortality;
> Chastised a little, they shall be greatly blessed,
> > because God tried them,
> > and found them worthy of himself.
> As gold in the furnace, he proved them,
> > and as sacrificial offerings he took them to himself.
> Those who trust in him shall understand truth,
> > and the faithful shall abide with him in love:
> Because grace and mercy are with his holy ones,
> > and his care is with his elect.

The word of the Lord.

C4   An unsullied life, the attainment of old age.

Wisdom 4:7–15
(1011-4)

A reading from the Book of Wisdom

> The just man, though he die early,
> > shall be at rest.
> For the age that is honorable comes not
> > with the passing of time,
> > nor can it be measured in terms of years.
> Rather, understanding is the hoary crown for men,
> > and an unsullied life, the attainment of old age.
> He who pleased God was loved;
> > he who lived among sinners was transported—
> Snatched away, lest wickedness pervert his mind
> > or deceit beguile his soul;
> For the witchery of paltry things obscures what is right
> > and the whirl of desire transforms the innocent mind.

Having become perfect in a short while,
    he reached the fullness of a long career;
for his soul was pleasing to the Lord,
    therefore he sped him out of the midst of wickedness.
But the people saw and did not understand,
    nor did they take this into account.

The word of the Lord.

C5   He will destroy death forever.

Isaiah 25:6a, 7–9
(1011-5)

A reading from the Book of the Prophet Isaiah

On this mountain the Lord of hosts
    will provide for all peoples.
On this mountain he will destroy
    the veil that veils all peoples,
The web that is woven over all nations;
    he will destroy death forever.
The Lord God will wipe away
    the tears from all faces;
The reproach of his people he will remove
    from the whole earth; for the Lord has spoken.

On that day it will be said:
"Behold our God, to whom we looked to save us!
    This is the Lord for whom we looked;
    let us rejoice and be glad that he has saved us!"

The word of the Lord.

C6   It is good to hope in silence for

Lamentations 3:17–26   the saving help of the Lord.
(1011-6)

A reading from the Book of Lamentations

My soul is deprived of peace,
    I have forgotten what happiness is;
I tell myself my future is lost,
    all that I hoped for from the Lord.

The thought of my homeless poverty
    is wormwood and gall;
Remembering it over and over
    leaves my soul downcast within me.
But I will call this to mind,
    as my reason to have hope:

The favors of the Lord are not exhausted,
    his mercies are not spent;
They are renewed each morning,
    so great is his faithfulness.
My portion is the Lord, says my soul;
    therefore will I hope in him.

Good is the Lord to one who waits for him,
    to the soul that seeks him;
It is good to hope in silence
    for the saving help of the Lord.

The word of the Lord.

C7

Daniel 12:1–3
(1011-7)

Many of those who sleep in the dust of the earth shall awake.

A reading from the Book of the Prophet Daniel

In those days, I, Daniel, mourned
    and heard this word of the Lord:
At that time there shall arise
    Michael, the great prince,
    guardian of your people;
It shall be a time unsurpassed in distress
    since nations began until that time.
At that time your people shall escape,
    everyone who is found written in the book.

Many of those who sleep
    in the dust of the earth shall awake;
Some shall live forever,
    others shall be an everlasting horror and disgrace.
But the wise shall shine brightly
    like the splendor of the firmament,
And those who lead the many to justice
    shall be like the stars forever.

The word of the Lord.

During Easter Time: New Testament

(Note: During the Easter season one of the following four readings is used as a
first reading instead of a passage from the Old Testament.)

C8

Long version:
Acts of the Apostles 10:34–43
(1012-1)

He is the one appointed by God as judge of the living and the dead.

A reading from the Acts of the Apostles

Peter proceeded to speak, saying:
"In truth, I see that God shows no partiality.
Rather, in every nation whoever fears him and acts uprightly
    is acceptable to him.
You know the word that he sent to the children of Israel
    as he proclaimed peace through Jesus Christ, who is Lord of all,
    what has happened all over Judea,
    beginning in Galilee after the baptism
    that John preached,
    how God anointed Jesus of Nazareth
    with the Holy Spirit and power.
He went about doing good
    and healing all those oppressed by the Devil,
    for God was with him.
We are witnesses of all that he did
    both in the country of the Jews and in Jerusalem.
They put him to death by hanging him on a tree.
This man God raised on the third day and granted that he be visible,
    not to all the people, but to us,
    the witnesses chosen by God in advance,
    who ate and drank with him after he rose from the dead.
He commissioned us to preach to the people
    and testify that he is the one appointed by God
    as judge of the living and the dead.
To him all the prophets bear witness,
    that everyone who believes in him
    will receive forgiveness of sins through his name."

The word of the Lord.

C8
Short version: Acts of the Apostles 10:34–36, 42–43

A reading from the Acts of the Apostles

>Peter proceeded to speak, saying:
>   "In truth, I see that God shows no partiality.
>Rather, in every nation whoever fears him and acts uprightly
>   is acceptable to him.
>You know the word that he sent to the children of Israel
>   as he proclaimed peace through Jesus Christ, who is Lord of all.
>He commissioned us to preach to the people
>   and testify that he is the one appointed by God
>   as judge of the living and the dead.
>To him all the prophets bear witness,
>   that everyone who believes in him
>   will receive forgiveness of sins through his name."

The word of the Lord.

C9   Blessed are the dead who die in the Lord.
Revelation 14:13
(1012-2)

A reading from the Book of Revelation

>I, John, heard a voice from heaven say, "Write this:
>   Blessed are the dead who die in the Lord from now on."
>"Yes," said the Spirit,
>   "let them find rest from their labors,
>   for their works accompany them."

The word of the Lord.

C10   The dead were judged according to their deeds.
Revelation 20:11–21:1
(1012-3)

A reading from the Book of Revelation

>I, John, saw a large white throne and the one who was sitting on it.
>The earth and the sky fled from his presence
>   and there was no place for them.

I saw the dead, the great and the lowly, standing before the throne,
  and scrolls were opened.
Then another scroll was opened, the book of life.
The dead were judged according to their deeds,
  by what was written in the scrolls.
The sea gave up its dead;
  then Death and Hades gave up their dead.
All the dead were judged according to their deeds.
Then Death and Hades were thrown into the pool of fire.
(This pool of fire is the second death.)
Anyone whose name was not found written in the book of life
  was thrown into the pool of fire.

Then I saw a new heaven and a new earth.
The former heaven and the former earth had passed away,
  and the sea was no more.

The word of the Lord.

C11 There shall be no more death.

Revelation 21:1–5a, 6b–7
(1012-4)

A reading from the Book of Revelation

I, John, saw a new heaven and a new earth.
The former heaven and the former earth had passed away,
  and the sea was no more.
I also saw the holy city, a new Jerusalem,
  coming down out of heaven from God,
  prepared as a bride adorned for her husband.
I heard a loud voice from the throne saying,
  "Behold, God's dwelling is with the human race.
He will dwell with them and they will be his people
  and God himself will always be with them as their God.
He will wipe every tear from their eyes,
  and there shall be no more death or mourning, wailing or pain,
  for the old order has passed away."

The One who sat on the throne said,
  "Behold, I make all things new.
I am the Alpha and the Omega,
  the beginning and the end.

To the thirsty I will give a gift
    from the spring of life-giving water.
The victor will inherit these gifts,
    and I shall be his God,
    and he will be my son."

The word of the Lord.

Responsorial Psalm

D1
Psalm 23:1–3, 4, 5, 6
(1013-1)

The Lord is my shepherd; there is nothing I shall want.
or:
Though I walk in the valley of darkness, I fear no evil, for you are with me.

> The Lord is my shepherd; I shall not want.
> In verdant pastures he gives me repose;
> Beside restful waters he leads me;
> he refreshes my soul.
> He guides me in right paths
> for his name's sake.

The Lord is my shepherd; there is nothing I shall want.
or:
Though I walk in the valley of darkness, I fear no evil, for you are with me.

> Even though I walk in the dark valley
> I fear no evil; for you are at my side
> With your rod and your staff
> that give me courage.

The Lord is my shepherd; there is nothing I shall want.
or:
Though I walk in the valley of darkness, I fear no evil, for you are with me.

> You spread the table before me
> in the sight of my foes;
> You anoint my head with oil;
> my cup overflows.

The Lord is my shepherd; there is nothing I shall want.
or:
Though I walk in the valley of darkness, I fear no evil, for you are with me.

> Only goodness and kindness follow me
> all the days of my life;
> And I shall dwell in the house of the Lord
> for years to come.

The Lord is my shepherd; there is nothing I shall want.
or:
Though I walk in the valley of darkness, I fear no evil, for you are with me.

D2

25:6 and 7b, 17–18, 20–21
(1013-2)

To you, O Lord, I lift my soul.
or:
No one who waits for you, O Lord, will ever be put to shame.

> Remember that your compassion, O LORD,
>   and your kindness are from of old.
> In your kindness remember me,
>   because of your goodness, O LORD.

To you, O Lord, I lift my soul.
or:
No one who waits for you, O Lord, will ever be put to shame.

> Relieve the troubles of my heart;
>   and bring me out of my distress.
> Put an end to my affliction and my suffering;
>   and take away all my sins.

To you, O Lord, I lift my soul.
or:
No one who waits for you, O Lord, will ever be put to shame.

> Preserve my life and rescue me;
>   let me not be put to shame, for I take refuge in you.
> Let integrity and uprightness preserve me,
>   because I wait for you, O LORD.

To you, O Lord, I lift my soul.
or:
No one who waits for you, O Lord, will ever be put to shame.

D3

27:1, 4, 7 and 8b and 9a, 13–14
(1013-3)

The Lord is my light and my salvation.
or:
I believe that I shall see the good things of the Lord in the land of the living.

The LORD is my light and my salvation;
   whom should I fear?
The LORD is my life's refuge;
   of whom should I be afraid?
The Lord is my light and my salvation.
or:
I believe that I shall see the good things of the Lord in the land of the living.

One thing I ask of the LORD;
   this I seek:
To dwell in the house of the LORD
   all the days of my life,
That I may gaze on the loveliness of the LORD
   and contemplate his temple.
The Lord is my light and my salvation.
or:
I believe that I shall see the good things of the Lord in the land of the living.

Hear, O LORD, the sound of my call;
   have pity on me, and answer me.
Your presence, O LORD, I seek.
   Hide not your face from me.
The Lord is my light and my salvation.
or:
I believe that I shall see the good things of the Lord in the land of the living.

I believe that I shall see the bounty of the LORD
   in the land of the living.
Wait for the LORD with courage;
   be stouthearted, and wait for the LORD.
The Lord is my light and my salvation.
or:
I believe that I shall see the good things of the Lord in the land of the living.

D4

42:2, 3, 5cdef; 43:3, 4, 5
(1013-4)

My soul is thirsting for the living God: when shall I see him face to face?

As the hind longs for the running waters,
    so my soul longs for you, O God.
My soul is thirsting for the living God: when shall I see him face to face?

Athirst is my soul for God, the living God.
    When shall I go and behold the face of God?
My soul is thirsting for the living God: when shall I see him face to face?

I went with the throng and led them in procession
    to the house of God.
Amid loud cries of joy and thanksgiving,
    with the multitude keeping festival.
My soul is thirsting for the living God: when shall I see him face to face?

Send forth your light and your fidelity;
    they shall lead me on
And bring me to your holy mountain,
    to your dwelling-place.
My soul is thirsting for the living God: when shall I see him face to face?

Then will I go in to the altar of God,
    the God of my gladness and joy;
Then will I give you thanks upon the harp,
    O God, my God!
My soul is thirsting for the living God: when shall I see him face to face?

Why are you so downcast, O my soul?
    Why do you sigh within me?
Hope in God! For I shall again be thanking him,
    in the presence of my savior and my God.
My soul is thirsting for the living God: when shall I see him face to face?

D5

63:2, 3–4, 5–6, 8–9
(1013-5)

My soul is thirsting for you, O Lord my God.

O God, you are my God whom I seek;
for you my flesh pines and my soul thirsts
like the earth, parched, lifeless and without water.
My soul is thirsting for you, O Lord my God.

Thus have I gazed toward you in the sanctuary
to see your power and your glory,
For your kindness is a greater good than life;
my lips shall glorify you.
My soul is thirsting for you, O Lord my God.

Thus will I bless you while I live;
lifting up my hands, I will call upon your name.
As with the riches of a banquet shall my soul be satisfied,
and with exultant lips my mouth shall praise you.
My soul is thirsting for you, O Lord my God.

You are my help,
and in the shadow of your wings I shout for joy.
My soul clings fast to you;
your right hand upholds me.
My soul is thirsting for you, O Lord my God.

D6

103:8 and 10, 13–14, 15–16, 17–18
(1013-6)

The Lord is kind and merciful.
or:
The salvation of the just comes from the Lord.

Merciful and gracious is the LORD,
slow to anger, and abounding in kindness.
Not according to our sins does he deal with us,
nor does he requite us according to our crimes.
The Lord is kind and merciful.

or:

The salvation of the just comes from the Lord.

> As a father has compassion on his children,
> > so the Lord has compassion on those who fear him.
> For he knows how we are formed,
> > he remembers that we are dust.

The Lord is kind and merciful.
or:
The salvation of the just comes from the Lord.

> Man's days are like those of grass;
> > like a flower of the field he blooms;
> The wind sweeps over him and he is gone,
> > and his place knows him no more.

The Lord is kind and merciful.
or:
The salvation of the just comes from the Lord.

> But the kindness of the Lord is from eternity
> > to eternity toward those who fear him,
> And his justice toward children's children
> > among those who keep his covenant
> > and remember to fulfill his precepts.

The Lord is kind and merciful.
or:
The salvation of the just comes from the Lord.

D7

116:5, 6, 10–11, 15–16ac
(1013-7)

I will walk in the presence of the Lord in the land of the living.
or:
Alleluia.

> Gracious is the Lord and just;
> > yes, our God is merciful.

I will walk in the presence of the Lord in the land of the living.

or:
Alleluia.

The LORD keeps the little ones;
I was brought low, and he saved me.
I will walk in the presence of the Lord in the land of the living.
or:
Alleluia.

I believed, even when I said,
"I am greatly afflicted";
I said in my alarm,
"No man is dependable."
I will walk in the presence of the Lord in the land of the living.
or:
Alleluia.

Precious in the eyes of the LORD
is the death of his faithful ones.
O LORD, I am your servant,
you have loosed my bonds.
I will walk in the presence of the Lord in the land of the living.
or:
Alleluia.

D8

122:1–2, 4–5, 6–7, 8–9
(1013-8)

I rejoiced when I heard them say: let us go to the house of the Lord.
or:
Let us go rejoicing to the house of the Lord.

I rejoiced because they said to me,
"We will go up to the house of the LORD."
And now we have set foot
within your gates, O Jerusalem.
I rejoiced when I heard them say: let us go to the house of the Lord.
or:
Let us go rejoicing to the house of the Lord.

To it the tribes go up,
the tribes of the LORD.
According to the decree for Israel,
to give thanks to the name of the LORD.

In it are set up judgment seats,
    seats for the house of David.
I rejoiced when I heard them say: let us go to the house of the Lord.
or:
Let us go rejoicing to the house of the Lord.

    Pray for the peace of Jerusalem!
        May those who love you prosper!
    May peace be within your walls,
        prosperity in your buildings.
I rejoiced when I heard them say: let us go to the house of the Lord.
or:
Let us go rejoicing to the house of the Lord.

    Because of my relatives and friends
        I will say, "Peace be within you!"
    Because of the house of the Lord, our God,
        I will pray for your good.
I rejoiced when I heard them say: let us go to the house of the Lord.
or:
Let us go rejoicing to the house of the Lord.

D9

130:1–2, 3–4, 5–6ab, 6c–7, 8
(1013-9)

Out of the depths, I cry to you, Lord.
or:
I hope in the Lord, I trust in his word.

    Out of the depths I cry to you, O Lord;
        Lord, hear my voice!
    Let your ears be attentive
        to my voice in supplication.
Out of the depths, I cry to you, Lord.

or:
I hope in the Lord, I trust in his word.

> If you, O Lord, mark iniquities,
>> Lord, who can stand?
> But with you is forgiveness,
>> that you may be revered.

Out of the depths, I cry to you, Lord.
or:
I hope in the Lord, I trust in his word.

> I trust in the Lord;
>> my soul trusts in his word.
> My soul waits for the Lord
>> more than the sentinels wait for the dawn.

Out of the depths, I cry to you, Lord.
or:
I hope in the Lord, I trust in his word.

> More than the sentinels wait for the dawn,
>> let Israel wait for the Lord,
> For with the Lord is kindness
>> and with him is plenteous redemption.

Out of the depths, I cry to you, Lord.
or:
I hope in the Lord, I trust in his word.

> And he will redeem Israel
>> from all their iniquities.

Out of the depths, I cry to you, Lord.
or:
I hope in the Lord, I trust in his word.

D10

143:1–2, 5–6, 7ab, 8ab, 10
(1013-10)

O Lord, hear my prayer.

> O Lord, hear my prayer;
>> hearken to my pleading in your faithfulness;
>> in your justice answer me.
> And enter not into judgment with your servant,
>> for before you no living man is just.

O Lord, hear my prayer.

> I remember the days of old;
>> I meditate on all your doings;
>> the works of your hands I ponder.
> I stretch out my hands to you;
>> my soul thirsts for you like parched land.

O Lord, hear my prayer.

> Hasten to answer me, O Lord;
>> for my spirit fails me.
> At dawn let me hear of your mercy,
>> for in you I trust.

O Lord, hear my prayer.

> Teach me to do your will,
>> for you are my God.
> May your good spirit guide me
>> on level ground.

O Lord, hear my prayer.

Second Reading

E1

Romans 5:5–11
(1014-1)

Since we are now justified by his Blood, we will be saved through him from the wrath.

A reading from the Letter of Saint Paul to the Romans

Brothers and sisters:
   Hope does not disappoint,
   because the love of God has been poured out into our hearts
   through the Holy Spirit who has been given to us.
For Christ, while we were still helpless,
   died at the appointed time for the ungodly.
Indeed, only with difficulty does one die for a just person,
   though perhaps for a good person
   one might even find courage to die.
But God proves his love for us
   in that while we were still sinners Christ died for us.
How much more then, since we are now justified by his Blood,
   will we be saved through him from the wrath.
Indeed, if, while we were enemies,
   we were reconciled to God through the death of his Son,
   how much more, once reconciled,
   will we be saved by his life.
Not only that,
   but we also boast of God through our Lord Jesus Christ,
   through whom we have now received reconciliation.

The word of the Lord.

E2 Where sin increased, grace overflowed all the more.

Romans 5:17–21
(1014-2)

A reading from the Letter of Saint Paul to the Romans

Brothers and sisters:
   If, by the transgression of the one,

death came to reign through that one,
how much more will those who receive the abundance of grace
and of the gift of justification
come to reign in life through the one Jesus Christ.
In conclusion, just as through one transgression
condemnation came upon all,
so, through one righteous act,
acquittal and life came to all.
For just as through the disobedience of the one man
the many were made sinners,
so through the obedience of the one
the many will be made righteous.
The law entered in so that transgression might increase
but, where sin increased, grace overflowed all the more, so that,
as sin reigned in death,
grace also might reign through justification for eternal life
through Jesus Christ our Lord.

The word of the Lord.

E3   We too might live in newness of life.

Long version: Romans 6:3–9
(1014-3)

A reading from the Letter of Saint Paul to the Romans

Brothers and sisters:
Are you unaware that we who were baptized into Christ Jesus
were baptized into his death?
We were indeed buried with him through baptism into death,
so that, just as Christ was raised from the dead
by the glory of the Father,
we too might live in newness of life.

For if we have grown into union with him through a death like his,
we shall also be united with him in the resurrection.
We know that our old self was crucified with him,
so that our sinful body might be done away with,
that we might no longer be in slavery to sin.
For a dead person has been absolved from sin.
If, then, we have died with Christ,
we believe that we shall also live with him.

We know that Christ, raised from the dead, dies no more;
    death no longer has power over him.

The word of the Lord.

E3

Short version: Romans 6:3–4, 8–9

A reading from the Letter of Saint Paul to the Romans

Brothers and sisters:
    Are you unaware that we who were baptized into Christ Jesus
    were baptized into his death?
We were indeed buried with him through baptism into death,
    so that, just as Christ was raised from the dead
    by the glory of the Father,
    we too might live in newness of life.

If, then, we have died with Christ,
    we believe that we shall also live with him.
We know that Christ, raised from the dead, dies no more;
    death no longer has power over him.

The word of the Lord.

E4

Romans 8:14–23
(1014-4)

We also groan within ourselves as we wait for adoption, the redemption of our bodies.

A reading from the Letter of Saint Paul to the Romans

Brothers and sisters:
    Those who are led by the Spirit of God are sons of God.
For you did not receive a spirit of slavery to fall back into fear,
    but you received a spirit of adoption,
    through which we cry, "*Abba*, Father!"
The Spirit itself bears witness with our spirit
    that we are children of God,
    and if children, then heirs,
    heirs of God and joint heirs with Christ,
    if only we suffer with him
    so that we may also be glorified with him.

I consider that the sufferings of this present time are as nothing
    compared with the glory to be revealed for us.
For creation awaits with eager expectation
    the revelation of the children of God;
    for creation was made subject to futility,
    not of its own accord but because of the one who subjected it,
    in hope that creation itself
    would be set free from slavery to corruption
    and share in the glorious freedom of the children of God.
We know that all creation is groaning in labor pains even until now;
    and not only that, but we ourselves,
    who have the firstfruits of the Spirit,
    we also groan within ourselves
    as we wait for adoption, the redemption of our bodies.

The word of the Lord.

E5   What will separate us from the love of Christ?

Romans 8:31b–35, 37–39
(1014-5)

A reading from the Letter of Saint Paul to the Romans

Brothers and sisters:
    If God is for us, who can be against us?
He did not spare his own Son
    but handed him over for us all,
    will he not also give us everything else along with him?
Who will bring a charge against God's chosen ones?
It is God who acquits us.
Who will condemn?
It is Christ Jesus who died, rather, was raised,
    who also is at the right hand of God,
    who indeed intercedes for us.
What will separate us from the love of Christ?
Will anguish, or distress or persecution, or famine,
    or nakedness, or peril, or the sword?

No, in all these things, we conquer overwhelmingly
    through him who loved us.
For I am convinced that neither death, nor life,
    nor angels, nor principalities,
    nor present things, nor future things,
    nor powers, nor height, nor depth,

nor any other creature will be able to separate us
from the love of God in Christ Jesus our Lord.

The word of the Lord.

E6   Whether we live or die, we are the Lord's.
Romans 14:7–9, 10c–12
(1014-6)

A reading from the Letter of Saint Paul to the Romans

Brothers and sisters:
    No one lives for oneself,
    and no one dies for oneself.
For if we live, we live for the Lord,
    and if we die, we die for the Lord;
    so then, whether we live or die, we are the Lord's.
For this is why Christ died and came to life,
    that he might be Lord of both the dead and the living.
Why then do you judge your brother?
Or you, why do you look down on your brother?
For we shall all stand before the judgment seat of God;
    for it is written:

    As I live, says the Lord, every knee shall bend before me,
        and every tongue shall give praise to God.

So then each of us shall give an accounting of himself to God.

The word of the Lord.

E7   So too in Christ shall all be brought to life.
Long version: 1 Corinthians 15:20–28
(1014-7)

A reading from the first Letter of Saint Paul to the Corinthians

Brothers and sisters:
    Christ has been raised from the dead,
    the firstfruits of those who have fallen asleep.
For since death came through a man,
    the resurrection of the dead came also through man.

For just as in Adam all die,
    so too in Christ shall all be brought to life,
    but each one in proper order:
    Christ the firstfruits;
    then, at his coming, those who belong to Christ;
    then comes the end,
    when he hands over the Kingdom to his God and Father.
For he must reign until he has put all his enemies under his feet.
The last enemy to be destroyed is death,
    for "he subjected everything under his feet."
But when it says that everything has been subjected,
    it is clear that it excludes the one who subjected everything to him.
When everything is subjected to him,
    then the Son himself will also be subjected
    to the one who subjected everything to him,
    so that God may be all in all.

The word of the Lord.

E7

Short version: 1 Corinthians 15:20–23

A reading from the first Letter of Saint Paul to the Corinthians

Brothers and sisters:
    Christ has been raised from the dead,
    the firstfruits of those who have fallen asleep.
For since death came through a man,
    the resurrection of the dead came also through man.
For just as in Adam all die,
    so too in Christ shall all be brought to life,
    but each one in proper order:
    Christ the firstfruits;
    then, at his coming, those who belong to Christ.

The word of the Lord.

E8
Death is swallowed up in victory.

1 Corinthians 15:51–57
(1014-8)

A reading from the first Letter of Saint Paul to the Corinthians

Brothers and sisters:
    Behold, I tell you a mystery.
We shall not all fall asleep, but we will all be changed,
    in an instant, in the blink of an eye, at the last trumpet.
For the trumpet will sound,
    the dead will be raised incorruptible,
    and we shall be changed.
For that which is corruptible must clothe itself with incorruptibility,
    and that which is mortal must clothe itself with immortality.
And when this which is corruptible clothes itself with incorruptibility
    and this which is mortal clothes itself with immortality,
    then the word that is written shall come about:

Death is swallowed up in victory.
Where, O death, is your victory?
Where, O death, is your sting?

The sting of death is sin,
    and the power of sin is the law.
But thanks be to God who gives us the victory
    through our Lord Jesus Christ.

The word of the Lord.

E9
**What is seen is transitory,
but what is unseen is eternal.**

2 Corinthians 4:14–5:1
(1014-9)

A reading from the second Letter of Saint Paul to the Corinthians

Brothers and sisters:
    We know that the One who raised the Lord Jesus
    will raise us also with Jesus
    and place us with you in his presence.
Everything indeed is for you,
    so that the grace bestowed in abundance on more and more people
    may cause the thanksgiving to overflow for the glory of God.

Therefore, we are not discouraged;
> rather, although our outer self is wasting away,
> our inner self is being renewed day by day.

For this momentary light affliction
> is producing for us an eternal weight of glory beyond all comparison,
> as we look not to what is seen but to what is unseen;
> for what is seen is transitory, but what is unseen is eternal.

For we know that if our earthly dwelling, a tent,
> should be destroyed,
> we have a building from God,
> a dwelling not made with hands,
> eternal in heaven.

The word of the Lord.

E10   We have a building from God, eternal in heaven.

2 Corinthians 5:1, 6–10
(1014-10)

A reading from the second Letter of Saint Paul to the Corinthians

Brothers and sisters:
> We know that if our earthly dwelling, a tent,
> should be destroyed,
> we have a building from God,
> a dwelling not made with hands,
> eternal in heaven.

We are always courageous,
> although we know that while we are at home in the body
> we are away from the Lord,
> for we walk by faith, not by sight.

Yet we are courageous,
> and we would rather leave the body and go home to the Lord.

Therefore, we aspire to please him,
> whether we are at home or away.

For we must all appear before the judgment seat of Christ,
> so that each may receive recompense,
> according to what he did in the body, whether good or evil.

The word of the Lord.

E11

Philippians 3:20–21
(1014-11)

He will change our lowly bodies to conform to his glory.

A reading from the Letter of Saint Paul to the Philippians

Brothers and sisters:
Our citizenship is in heaven,
and from it we also await a savior, the Lord Jesus Christ.
He will change our lowly body
to conform with his glorified Body
by the power that enables him also
to bring all things into subjection to himself.

The word of the Lord.

E12

1 Thessalonians 4:13–18
(1014-12)

Thus we shall always be with the Lord.

A reading from the first Letter of Saint Paul to the Thessalonians

We do not want you to be unaware, brothers and sisters,
about those who have fallen asleep,
so that you may not grieve like the rest, who have no hope.
For if we believe that Jesus died and rose,
so too will God, through Jesus,
bring with him those who have fallen asleep.
Indeed, we tell you this, on the word of the Lord,
that we who are alive,
who are left until the coming of the Lord,
will surely not precede those who have fallen asleep.
For the Lord himself, with a word of command,
with the voice of an archangel and with the trumpet of God,
will come down from heaven,
and the dead in Christ will rise first.
Then we who are alive, who are left,
will be caught up together with them in the clouds
to meet the Lord in the air.
Thus we shall always be with the Lord.
Therefore, console one another with these words.

The word of the Lord.

E13   If we have died with him we shall also live with him.

2 Timothy 2:8–13
(1014-13)

A reading from the second Letter of Saint Paul to Timothy

Beloved:
Remember Jesus Christ, raised from the dead, a descendant of
    David:
such is my Gospel, for which I am suffering,
even to the point of chains, like a criminal.
But the word of God is not chained.
Therefore, I bear with everything for the sake of those who are chosen,
so that they too may obtain the salvation that is in Christ Jesus,
together with eternal glory.
This saying is trustworthy:
If we have died with him
    we shall also live with him;
if we persevere
    we shall also reign with him.
But if we deny him
    he will deny us.
If we are unfaithful
    he remains faithful,
    for he cannot deny himself.

The word of the Lord.

E14   We shall see him as he is.

1 John 3:1–2
(1014-14)

A reading from the first Letter of Saint John

Beloved:
See what love the Father has bestowed on us
that we may be called the children of God.
Yet so we are.
The reason the world does not know us
is that it did not know him.
Beloved, we are God's children now;
what we shall be has not yet been revealed.

We do know that when it is revealed we shall be like him,
for we shall see him as he is.

The word of the Lord.

E15

1 John 3:14–16
(1014-15)

We know that we have passed from death to life because we love our brothers.

A reading from the first Letter of Saint John

Beloved:
We know that we have passed from death to life
because we love our brothers.
Whoever does not love remains in death.
Everyone who hates his brother is a murderer,
and you know that no murderer has eternal life remaining in him.
The way we came to know love
was that he laid down his life for us;
so we ought to lay down our lives for our brothers.

The word of the Lord.

Alleluia Verse and Verse before the Gospel

F1

See Matthew 11:25

(1015-1)

> Blessed are you, Father, Lord of heaven and earth;
> you have revealed to the childlike the mysteries of the Kingdom.

F2

Matthew 25:34

(1015-2)

> Come, you who are blessed by my Father, says the Lord;
> inherit the kingdom prepared for you from the foundation of the
> world.

F3

John 3:16

(1015-3)

> God so loved the world that he gave his only-begotten Son,
> so that everyone who believes in him might have eternal life.

F4

John 6:39

(1015-4)

> This is the will of my Father, says the Lord,
> that I should lose nothing of all that he has given to me,
> and that I should raise it up on the last day.

F5

John 6:40
(1015-5)

> This is the will of my Father, says the Lord,
> that everyone who sees the Son and believes in him may have
> eternal life,
> and I shall raise him on the last day.

F6

John 6:51
(1015-6)

> I am the living bread that came down from heaven,
> says the Lord;
> whoever eats this bread will live forever.

F7

John 11:25a, 26
(1015-7)

> I am the resurrection and the life, says the Lord;
> whoever believes in me will never die.

F8

See Philippians 3:20
(1015-8)

> Our true home is in heaven,
> and Jesus Christ, whose return we long for,
> will come from heaven to save us.

F9

2 Timothy 2:11–12a
(1015-9)

> If we die with Christ, we shall live with him,
> and if we persevere we shall also reign with him.

F10

Revelation 1:5a, 6b
(1015-10)

> Jesus Christ is the firstborn from the dead;
> glory and power be his forever and ever. Amen.

F11

Revelation 14:13
(1015-11)

> Blessed are those who have died in the Lord;
> let them rest from their labors for their good deeds go with them.

Gospel Reading

G1

Matthew 5:1–12a

(1016-1)

**Rejoice and be glad, for your
reward will be great in heaven.**

✠ A reading from the holy Gospel according to Matthew

When Jesus saw the crowds, he went up the mountain,
    and after he had sat down, his disciples came to him.
He began to teach them, saying:
    "Blessed are the poor in spirit,
        for theirs is the Kingdom of heaven.
    Blessed are they who mourn,
        for they will be comforted.
    Blessed are the meek,
        for they will inherit the land.
    Blessed are they who hunger and thirst for righteousness,
        for they will be satisfied.
    Blessed are the merciful,
        for they will be shown mercy.
    Blessed are the clean of heart,
        for they will see God.
    Blessed are the peacemakers,
        for they will be called children of God.
    Blessed are they who are persecuted for the sake of righteousness,
        for theirs is the Kingdom of heaven.
    Blessed are you when they insult you and persecute you
        and utter every kind of evil against you falsely because of me.
    Rejoice and be glad,
        for your reward will be great in heaven."

The Gospel of the Lord.

G2   Come to me and I will give you rest.
Matthew 11:25–30
(1016-2)

✝ A reading from the holy Gospel according to Matthew

At that time Jesus answered:
"I give praise to you, Father, Lord of heaven and earth,
for although you have hidden these things
from the wise and the learned
you have revealed them to the childlike.
Yes, Father, such has been your gracious will.
All things have been handed over to me by my Father.
No one knows the Son except the Father,
and no one knows the Father except the Son
and anyone to whom the Son wishes to reveal him.

"Come to me, all you who labor and are burdened,
and I will give you rest.
Take my yoke upon you and learn from me,
for I am meek and humble of heart;
and you will find rest for yourselves.
For my yoke is easy, and my burden light."

The Gospel of the Lord.

G3   Behold the bridegroom! Come out to him!
Matthew 25:1–13
(1016-3)

✝ A reading from the holy Gospel according to Matthew

Jesus told his disciples this parable:
"The Kingdom of heaven will be like ten virgins
who took their lamps and went out to meet the bridegroom.
Five of them were foolish and five were wise.
The foolish ones, when taking their lamps,
brought no oil with them,
but the wise brought flasks of oil with their lamps.
Since the bridegroom was long delayed,
they all became drowsy and fell asleep.
At midnight, there was a cry,
'Behold, the bridegroom! Come out to meet him!'

Then all those virgins got up and trimmed their lamps.
The foolish ones said to the wise,
    'Give us some of your oil,
    for our lamps are going out.'
But the wise ones replied,
    'No, for there may not be enough for us and you.
Go instead to the merchants and buy some for yourselves.'
While they went off to buy it,
    the bridegroom came
    and those who were ready went into the wedding feast with him.
Then the door was locked.
Afterwards the other virgins came and said,
    'Lord, Lord, open the door for us!'
But he said in reply,
    'Amen, I say to you, I do not know you.'
Therefore, stay awake,
    for you know neither the day nor the hour."

The Gospel of the Lord.

G4   Come, you who are blessed by my Father.

Matthew 25:31–46
(1016-4)

✠ **A reading from the holy Gospel according to Matthew**

Jesus said to his disciples:
    "When the Son of Man comes in his glory,
    and all the angels with him,
    he will sit upon his glorious throne,
    and all the nations will be assembled before him.
And he will separate them one from another,
    as a shepherd separates the sheep from the goats.
He will place the sheep on his right and the goats on his left.
Then the king will say to those on his right,
    'Come, you who are blessed by my Father.
Inherit the kingdom prepared for you from the foundation of the world.
For I was hungry and you gave me food,
    I was thirsty and you gave me drink,
    a stranger and you welcomed me,
    naked and you clothed me,

ill and you cared for me,
in prison and you visited me.'
Then the righteous will answer him and say,
'Lord, when did we see you hungry and feed you,
or thirsty and give you drink?
When did we see you a stranger and welcome you,
or naked and clothe you?
When did we see you ill or in prison, and visit you?'
And the king will say to them in reply,
'Amen, I say to you, whatever you did
for one of these least brothers of mine, you did for me.'
Then he will say to those on his left,
'Depart from me, you accursed,
into the eternal fire prepared for the Devil and his angels.
For I was hungry and you gave me no food,
I was thirsty and you gave me no drink,
a stranger and you gave me no welcome,
naked and you gave me no clothing,
ill and in prison, and you did not care for me.'
Then they will answer and say,
'Lord, when did we see you hungry or thirsty
or a stranger or naked or ill or in prison,
and not minister to your needs?'
He will answer them, 'Amen, I say to you,
what you did not do for one of these least ones,
you did not do for me.'
And these will go off to eternal punishment,
but the righteous to eternal life."

The Gospel of the Lord.

G5   Jesus gave a loud cry and breathed his last.

Long version: Mark 15:33–39; 16:1–6
(1016-5)

✠ **A reading from the holy Gospel according to Mark**

At noon darkness came over the whole land
until three in the afternoon.
And at three o'clock Jesus cried out in a loud voice,
"*Eloi, Eloi, lema sabachthani?*"

which is translated,
    "My God, my God, why have you forsaken me?"
Some of the bystanders who heard it said,
    "Look, he is calling Elijah."
One of them ran, soaked a sponge with wine, put it on a reed,
    and gave it to him to drink, saying,
    "Wait, let us see if Elijah comes to take him down."
Jesus gave a loud cry and breathed his last.
The veil of the sanctuary was torn in two from top to bottom.
When the centurion who stood facing him
    saw how he breathed his last he said,
    "Truly this man was the Son of God!"

When the sabbath was over,
    Mary Magdalene, Mary, the mother of James, and Salome
    bought spices so that they might go and anoint him.
Very early when the sun had risen,
    on the first day of the week, they came to the tomb.
They were saying to one another,
    "Who will roll back the stone for us
    from the entrance to the tomb?"
When they looked up,
    they saw that the stone had been rolled back;
    it was very large.
On entering the tomb they saw a young man
    sitting on the right side, clothed in a white robe,
    and they were utterly amazed.
He said to them, "Do not be amazed!
You seek Jesus of Nazareth, the crucified.
He has been raised; he is not here.
Behold the place where they laid him."

The Gospel of the Lord.

G5

Short version: Mark 15:33–39

+ A reading from the holy Gospel according to Mark

    At noon darkness came over the whole land
        until three in the afternoon.
    And at three o'clock Jesus cried out in a loud voice,
        "Eloi, Eloi, lema sabachthani?"

which is translated,
    "My God, my God, why have you forsaken me?"
Some of the bystanders who heard it said,
    "Look, he is calling Elijah."
One of them ran, soaked a sponge with wine, put it on a reed,
    and gave it to him to drink, saying,
    "Wait, let us see if Elijah comes to take him down."
Jesus gave a loud cry and breathed his last.
The veil of the sanctuary was torn in two from top to bottom.
When the centurion who stood facing him
    saw how he breathed his last he said,
    "Truly this man was the Son of God!"

The Gospel of the Lord.

G6   Young man, I tell you, arise!
Luke 7:11–17
(1016-6)

✟ A reading from the holy Gospel according to Luke

Jesus journeyed to a city called Nain,
    and his disciples and a large crowd accompanied him.
As he drew near to the gate of the city,
    a man who had died was being carried out,
    the only son of his mother, and she was a widow.
A large crowd from the city was with her.
When the Lord saw her,
    he was moved with pity for her and said to her,
    "Do not weep."
He stepped forward and touched the coffin;
    at this the bearers halted,
    and he said, "Young man, I tell you, arise!"
The dead man sat up and began to speak,
    and Jesus gave him to his mother.
Fear seized them all, and they glorified God, exclaiming,
    "A great prophet has arisen in our midst,"
    and "God has visited his people."
This report about him spread through the whole of Judea
    and in all the surrounding region.

The Gospel of the Lord.

G7   You also must be prepared.
Luke 12:35–40
(1016-7)

✟ A reading from the holy Gospel according to Luke

Jesus said to his disciples:
    "Gird your loins and light your lamps
    and be like servants who await their master's return from a wedding,
    ready to open immediately when he comes and knocks.
Blessed are those servants
    whom the master finds vigilant on his arrival.
Amen, I say to you, he will gird himself,
    have them recline at table, and proceed to wait on them.
And should he come in the second or third watch
    and find them prepared in this way,
    blessed are those servants.
Be sure of this:
    if the master of the house had known the hour
    when the thief was coming,
    he would not have let his house be broken into.
You also must be prepared, for at an hour you do not expect,
    the Son of Man will come."

The Gospel of the Lord.

G8   Today you will be with me in Paradise.
Luke 23:33, 39–43
(1016-8)

✟ A reading from the holy Gospel according to Luke

When the soldiers came to the place called the Skull,
    they crucified Jesus and the criminals there,
    one on his right, the other on his left.

Now one of the criminals hanging there
    reviled Jesus, saying,
    "Are you not the Christ?
    Save yourself and us."
The other man, however, rebuking him, said in reply,
    "Have you no fear of God,
    for you are subject to the same condemnation?

And indeed, we have been condemned justly,
for the sentence we received corresponds to our crimes,
but this man has done nothing criminal."
Then he said,
"Jesus, remember me when you come into your Kingdom."
He replied to him,
"Amen, I say to you,
today you will be with me in Paradise."
The Gospel of the Lord.

G9   Father, into your hands I commend my spirit.

Long version: Luke 23:44–46, 50, 52–53; 24:1–6a
(1016-9)

✟ **A reading from the holy Gospel according to Luke**

It was about noon and darkness came over the whole land
until three in the afternoon
because of an eclipse of the sun.
Then the veil of the temple was torn down the middle.
Jesus cried out in a loud voice,
"Father, into your hands I commend my spirit";
and when he had said this he breathed his last.

Now there was a virtuous and righteous man named Joseph who,
though he was a member of the council,
went to Pilate and asked for the Body of Jesus.
After he had taken the Body down,
he wrapped it in a linen cloth
and laid him in a rock-hewn tomb
in which no one had yet been buried.

At daybreak on the first day of the week
the women took the spices they had prepared
and went to the tomb.
They found the stone rolled away from the tomb;
but when they entered,
they did not find the Body of the Lord Jesus.
While they were puzzling over this, behold,
two men in dazzling garments appeared to them.
They were terrified and bowed their faces to the ground.

They said to them,
> "Why do you seek the living one among the dead?
> He is not here, but he has been raised."

The Gospel of the Lord.

G9
Short version: Luke 23:44–46, 50, 52–53

✝ A reading from the holy Gospel according to Luke

It was about noon and darkness came over the whole land
> until three in the afternoon
> because of an eclipse of the sun.
Then the veil of the temple was torn down the middle.
Jesus cried out in a loud voice,
> "Father, into your hands I commend my spirit";
> and when he had said this he breathed his last.

Now there was a virtuous and righteous man named Joseph who,
> though he was a member of the council,
> went to Pilate and asked for the Body of Jesus.
After he had taken the Body down,
> he wrapped it in a linen cloth
> and laid him in a rock-hewn tomb
> in which no one had yet been buried.

The Gospel of the Lord.

G10   Was it not necessary that the Christ should suffer
Long version: Luke 24:13–35   these things and enter into his glory?
(1016-10)

✝ A reading from the holy Gospel according to Luke

That very day, the first day of the week,
> two of the disciples of Jesus were going
> to a village called Emmaus, seven miles from Jerusalem,
> and they were conversing about all the things that had occurred.

And it happened that while they were conversing and debating,
 Jesus himself drew near and walked with them,
 but their eyes were prevented from recognizing him.
He asked them,
 "What are you discussing as you walk along?"
They stopped, looking downcast.
One of them, named Cleopas, said to him in reply,
 "Are you the only visitor to Jerusalem
 who does not know of the things
 that have taken place there in these days?"
And he replied to them, "What sort of things?"
They said to him,
 "The things that happened to Jesus the Nazarene,
 who was a prophet mighty in deed and word
 before God and all the people,
 how our chief priests and rulers both handed him over
 to a sentence of death and crucified him.
But we were hoping that he would be the one to redeem Israel;
 and besides all this,
 it is now the third day since this took place.
Some women from our group, however, have astounded us:
 they were at the tomb early in the morning
 and did not find his Body;
 they came back and reported
 that they had indeed seen a vision of angels
 who announced that he was alive.
Then some of those with us went to the tomb
 and found things just as the women had described,
 but him they did not see."
And he said to them, "Oh, how foolish you are!
How slow of heart to believe all that the prophets spoke!
Was it not necessary that the Christ should suffer these things
 and enter into his glory?"
Then beginning with Moses and all the prophets,
 Jesus interpreted to them what referred to him
 in all the Scriptures.
As they approached the village to which they were going,
 Jesus gave the impression that he was going on farther.
But they urged him, "Stay with us,
 for it is nearly evening and the day is almost over."
So he went in to stay with them.
And it happened that, while he was with them at table,
 he took bread, said the blessing,
 broke it, and gave it to them.

With that their eyes were opened and they recognized him,
    but he vanished from their sight.
Then they said to each other,
    "Were not our hearts burning within us
    while he spoke to us on the way and opened the Scriptures to us?"
So they set out at once and returned to Jerusalem
    where they found gathered together
    the Eleven and those with them, who were saying,
    "The Lord has truly been raised and has appeared to Simon!"
Then the two recounted
    what had taken place on the way
    and how he was made known to them in the breaking of the bread.

The Gospel of the Lord.

G10

Short version: Luke 24:13–16, 28–35

✝ A reading from the holy Gospel according to Luke

That very day, the first day of the week,
    two of the disciples of Jesus were going
    to a village called Emmaus, seven miles from Jerusalem,
    and they were conversing about all the things that had occurred.
And it happened that while they were conversing and debating,
    Jesus himself drew near and walked with them,
    but their eyes were prevented from recognizing him.
As they approached the village to which they were going,
    he gave the impression that he was going on farther.
But they urged him, "Stay with us,
    for it is nearly evening and the day is almost over."
So he went in to stay with them.
And it happened that, while he was with them at table,
    he took bread, said the blessing,
    broke it, and gave it to them.
With that their eyes were opened and they recognized him,
    but he vanished from their sight.
Then they said to each other,
    "Were not our hearts burning within us
    while he spoke to us on the way and opened the Scriptures to us?"
So they set out at once and returned to Jerusalem
    where they found gathered together

the Eleven and those with them, who were saying,
"The Lord has truly been raised and has appeared to Simon!"
Then the two recounted
what had taken place on the way
and how he was made known to them in the breaking of the bread.

The Gospel of the Lord.

G11

John 5:24–29
(1016-11)

Whoever hears my word and believes has passed from death to life.

✟ A reading from the holy Gospel according to John

Jesus answered the Jews and said to them:
"Amen, amen, I say to you, whoever hears my word
    and believes in the one who sent me
    has eternal life and will not come to condemnation,
    but has passed from death to life.
Amen, amen, I say to you, the hour is coming and is now here
    when the dead will hear the voice of the Son of God,
    and those who hear will live.
For just as the Father has life in himself,
    so also he gave to the Son the possession of life in himself.
And he gave him power to exercise judgment,
    because he is the Son of Man.
Do not be amazed at this,
    because the hour is coming in which all who are in the tombs
    will hear his voice and will come out,
    those who have done good deeds
    to the resurrection of life,
    but those who have done wicked deeds
    to the resurrection of condemnation."

The Gospel of the Lord.

G12
John 6:37–40
(1016-12)

Everyone who sees the Son and believes in him may have eternal life and I shall raise him on the last day.

✝ A reading from the holy Gospel according to John

Jesus said to the crowds:
"Everything that the Father gives me will come to me,
and I will not reject anyone who comes to me,
because I came down from heaven not to do my own will
but the will of the one who sent me.
And this is the will of the one who sent me,
that I should not lose anything of what he gave me,
but that I should raise it on the last day.
For this is the will of my Father,
that everyone who sees the Son and believes in him
may have eternal life,
and I shall raise him on the last day."

The Gospel of the Lord.

G13
John 6:51–59
(1016-13)

Whoever eats this bread will live forever, and I will raise them up on the last day.

✝ A reading from the holy Gospel according to John

Jesus said to the crowds:
"I am the living bread that came down from heaven;
whoever eats this bread will live forever;
and the bread that I will give is my Flesh
for the life of the world."

The Jews quarreled among themselves, saying,
"How can this man give us his Flesh to eat?"
Jesus said to them,
"Amen, amen, I say to you,
unless you eat the Flesh of the Son of Man and drink his Blood,
you do not have life within you.
Whoever eats my Flesh and drinks my Blood
has eternal life,
and I will raise him on the last day.

For my Flesh is true food,
   and my Blood is true drink.
Whoever eats my Flesh and drinks my Blood
   remains in me and I in him.
Just as the living Father sent me
   and I have life because of the Father,
   so also the one who feeds on me
   will have life because of me.
This is the bread that came down from heaven.
Unlike your ancestors who ate and still died,
   whoever eats this bread will live forever."

The Gospel of the Lord.

G14   I am the resurrection and the life.
Long version: John 11:17–27
(1016-14)

✠ **A reading from the holy Gospel according to John**

When Jesus arrived in Bethany, he found that Lazarus
   had already been in the tomb for four days.
Now Bethany was near Jerusalem, only about two miles away.
Many of the Jews had come to Martha and Mary
   to comfort them about their brother.
When Martha heard that Jesus was coming,
   she went to meet him;
   but Mary sat at home.
Martha said to Jesus,
   "Lord, if you had been here,
   my brother would not have died.
But even now I know that whatever you ask of God,
   God will give you."
Jesus said to her,
   "Your brother will rise."
Martha said to him,
   "I know he will rise,
   in the resurrection on the last day."
Jesus told her,
   "I am the resurrection and the life;
   whoever believes in me, even if he dies, will live,
   and everyone who lives and believes in me will never die.
Do you believe this?"
She said to him, "Yes, Lord.

I have come to believe that you are the Christ, the Son of God,
the one who is coming into the world."

The Gospel of the Lord.

G14

Short version: John 11:21–27

✟ **A reading from the holy Gospel according to John**

Martha said to Jesus,
"Lord, if you had been here,
my brother would not have died.
But even now I know that whatever you ask of God,
God will give you."
Jesus said to her,
"Your brother will rise."
Martha said to him,
"I know he will rise,
in the resurrection on the last day."
Jesus told her,
"I am the resurrection and the life;
whoever believes in me, even if he dies, will live,
and everyone who lives and believes in me will never die.
Do you believe this?"
She said to him, "Yes, Lord.
I have come to believe that you are the Christ, the Son of God,
the one who is coming into the world."

The Gospel of the Lord.

G15   Lazarus, come out!

John 11:32–45
(1016-15)

✟ **A reading from the holy Gospel according to John**

When Mary came to where Jesus was and saw him,
she fell at his feet and said to him,
"Lord, if you had been here,
my brother would not have died."
When Jesus saw her weeping and the Jews who had come with her
weeping,

he became perturbed and deeply troubled, and said,
        "Where have you laid him?"
They said to him, "Sir, come and see."
And Jesus wept.
So the Jews said, "See how he loved him."
But some of them said,
        "Could not the one who opened the eyes of the blind man
        have done something so that this man would not have died?"

So Jesus, perturbed again, came to the tomb.
It was a cave, and a stone lay across it.
Jesus said, "Take away the stone."
Martha, the dead man's sister, said to him,
        "Lord, by now there will be a stench;
        he has been dead for four days."
Jesus said to her,
        "Did I not tell you that if you believe
        you will see the glory of God?"
So they took away the stone.
And Jesus raised his eyes and said,
        "Father, I thank you for hearing me.
I know that you always hear me;
        but because of the crowd here I have said this,
        that they may believe that you sent me."
And when he had said this,
        he cried out in a loud voice,
        "Lazarus, come out!"
The dead man came out,
        tied hand and foot with burial bands,
        and his face was wrapped in a cloth.
So Jesus said to the crowd,
        "Untie him and let him go."

Now many of Jews who had come to Mary
        and seen what he had done began to believe in him.

The Gospel of the Lord.

G16   If it dies, it produces much fruit.

Long version: John 12:23–28
(1016-16)

✟ A reading from the holy Gospel according to John

Jesus said to his disciples:
    "The hour has come for the Son of Man to be glorified.
Amen, amen, I say to you,
    unless a grain of wheat falls to the ground and dies,
    it remains just a grain of wheat;
    but if it dies, it produces much fruit.
Whoever loves his life will lose it,
    and whoever hates his life in this world
    will preserve it for eternal life.
Whoever serves me must follow me,
    and where I am, there also will my servant be.
The Father will honor whoever serves me.

"I am troubled now. Yet what should I say?
'Father, save me from this hour'?
But it was for this purpose that I came to this hour.
Father, glorify your name."
Then a voice came from heaven,
    "I have glorified it and will glorify it again."

The Gospel of the Lord.

G16

Short version: John 12:23–26

✟ A reading from the holy Gospel according to John

Jesus said to his disciples:
    "The hour has come for the Son of Man to be glorified.
Amen, amen, I say to you,
    unless a grain of wheat falls to the ground and dies,
    it remains just a grain of wheat;
    but if it dies, it produces much fruit.
Whoever loves his life will lose it,
    and whoever hates his life in this world
    will preserve it for eternal life.

Whoever serves me must follow me,
  and where I am, there also will my servant be.
The Father will honor whoever serves me."

The Gospel of the Lord.

G17 In my Father's house there are many dwellings.

John 14:1–6
(1016-17)

✠ A reading from the holy Gospel according to John

Jesus said to his disciples:
  "Do not let your hearts be troubled.
You have faith in God; have faith also in me.
In my Father's house there are many dwelling places.
If there were not,
  would I have told you that I am going to prepare a place for you?
And if I go and prepare a place for you,
  I will come back again and take you to myself,
  so that where I am you also may be.
Where I am going you know the way."
Thomas said to him,
  "Master, we do not know where you are going;
  how can we know the way?"
Jesus said to him, "I am the way and the truth and the life.
No one comes to the Father except through me."

The Gospel of the Lord.

G18 I wish that where I am they also may be with me.

John 17:24–26
(1016-18)

✠ A reading from the holy Gospel according to John

Jesus raised his eyes to heaven and said:
  "Father, those whom you gave me are your gift to me.
I wish that where I am they also may be with me,
  that they may see my glory that you gave me,
  because you loved me before the foundation of the world.

Righteous Father, the world also does not know you,
  but I know you, and they know that you sent me.
I made known to them your name and I will make it known,
  that the love with which you loved me
  may be in them and I in them."

The Gospel of the Lord.

G19   And bowing his head he handed over his Spirit.

John 19:17–18, 25–39
(1016-19)

✝ **A reading from the holy Gospel according to John**

So they took Jesus, and, carrying the cross himself,
  he went out to what is called the Place of the Skull,
  in Hebrew, Golgotha.
There they crucified him, and with him two others,
  one on either side, with Jesus in the middle.

Standing by the cross of Jesus were his mother
  and his mother's sister, Mary the wife of Clopas,
  and Mary Magdalene.
When Jesus saw his mother and the disciple whom he loved,
  he said to his mother, "Woman, behold, your son."
Then he said to the disciple,
  "Behold, your mother."
And from that hour the disciple took her into his home.

After this, aware that everything was now finished,
  in order that the Scripture might be fulfilled,
  Jesus said, "I thirst."
There was a vessel filled with common wine.
So they put a sponge soaked in wine on a sprig of hyssop
  and put it up to his mouth.
When Jesus had taken the wine, he said, "It is finished."
And bowing his head, he handed over the Spirit.

Now since it was preparation day,
  in order that the bodies might not remain on the cross on the
    sabbath,
  for the sabbath day of that week was a solemn one,

the Jews asked Pilate that their legs be broken
   and they be taken down.
So the soldiers came and broke the legs of the first
   and then of the other one who was crucified with Jesus.
But when they came to Jesus and saw that he was already dead,
   they did not break his legs,
   but one soldier thrust his lance into his side,
   and immediately Blood and water flowed out.
An eyewitness has testified, and his testimony is true;
   he knows that he is speaking the truth,
   so that you also may come to believe.
For this happened so that the Scripture passage might be fulfilled:
   Not a bone of it will be broken.
And again another passage says:
   They will look upon him whom they have pierced.

After this, Joseph of Arimathea,
   secretly a disciple of Jesus for fear of the Jews,
   asked Pilate if he could remove the Body of Jesus.
And Pilate permitted it.
So he came and took his Body.
Nicodemus, the one who had first come to him at night,
   also came bringing a mixture of myrrh and aloes
   weighing about one hundred pounds.

The Gospel of the Lord.

General Intercessions

You may use one of the following formulas, combine parts of several together, adapt the material below to your circumstances, or compose one of your own.

If you choose to write your own, those given here can serve as helpful models. The various intentions should express the congregation's prayerful concern not only for those gathered for the funeral but also for others in particular need throughout the world.

Record your choices on the selection form using the page number and the letter-number code on the left side of each heading.

H1 (OCF, 167-A)

The Priest begins:

> Brothers and sisters, Jesus Christ is risen from the dead and sits at the right hand of the Father, where he intercedes for his Church. Confident that God hears the voices of those who trust in the Lord Jesus, we join our prayers to his:

Assisting minister:

> In baptism N. received the light of Christ. Scatter the darkness now and lead him (her) over the waters of death.
>
> Lord, in your mercy:
> R. Hear our prayer.

Assisting minister:

> Our brother/sister N. was nourished at the table of the Savior. Welcome him (her) into the halls of the heavenly banquet.
>
> Lord, in your mercy:
> R. Hear our prayer.

For a Religious

Assisting minister:

> Our brother/sister N. spent his (her) life following Jesus, poor, chaste, and obedient. Count him (her) among all holy men and women who sing in your courts.
>
> Lord, in your mercy:
> R. Hear our prayer.

For a Bishop or Priest

Assisting minister:

Our brother N. shared in the priesthood of Jesus Christ,
leading God's people in prayer and worship.
Bring him into your presence where he will take his place in
the heavenly liturgy.

Lord, in your mercy:
R. Hear our prayer.

For a Deacon

Assisting minister:

Our brother N. served God's people as a deacon of the Church.
Prepare a place for him in the kingdom whose coming he
proclaimed.

Lord, in your mercy:
R. Hear our prayer.

Assisting minister:

Many friends and members of our families have gone before
us and await the kingdom. Grant them an everlasting home
with your Son.

Lord, in your mercy:
R. Hear our prayer.

Assisting minister:

Many people die by violence, war, and famine each day. Show
your mercy to those who suffer so unjustly these sins against
your love, and gather them to the eternal kingdom of peace.

Lord, in your mercy:
R. Hear our prayer.

Assisting minister:

Those who trusted in the Lord now sleep in the Lord. Give
refreshment, rest, and peace to all whose faith is known to
you alone.

Lord, in your mercy:
R. Hear our prayer.

For the mourners

Assisting minister:

The family and friends of N. seek comfort and consolation. Heal their pain and dispel the darkness and doubt that come from grief.

Lord, in your mercy:
R. Hear our prayer.

Assisting minister:

We are assembled here in faith and confidence to pray for our brother/sister N. Strengthen our hope so that we may live in the expectation of your Son's coming.

Lord, in your mercy:
R. Hear our prayer.

The Priest then concludes:

Lord God,
giver of peace and healer of souls,
hear the prayers of the Redeemer, Jesus Christ,
and the voices of your people,
whose lives were purchased by the blood of the Lamb.
Forgive the sins of all who sleep in Christ
and grant them a place in the kingdom.

We ask this through Christ our Lord.
R. Amen.

H2 (OCF, 167-B)

The Priest begins:

God, the almighty Father, raised Christ his Son from the dead; with confidence we ask him to save all his people, living and dead:

Assisting minister:

For N. who in baptism was given the pledge of eternal life, that he (she) may now be admitted to the company of the saints.

We pray to the Lord.
R. Lord, hear our prayer.

Assisting minister:
> For our brother/sister who ate the body of Christ, the bread of life, that he (she) may be raised up on the last day.

> **We pray to the Lord.**
> R. Lord, hear our prayer.

For a deacon

Assisting minister:
> For our brother N., who proclaimed the Good News of Jesus Christ and served the needs of the poor, that he may be welcomed into the sanctuary of heaven.

> **We pray to the Lord.**
> R. Lord, hear our prayer.

For a bishop or priest

Assisting minister:
> For our brother N., who served the Church as a bishop/priest, that he may be given a place in the liturgy of heaven.

> **We pray to the Lord.**
> R. Lord, hear our prayer.

Assisting minister:
> For our deceased relatives and friends and for all who have helped us, that they may have the reward of their goodness.

> **We pray to the Lord.**
> R. Lord, hear our prayer.

Assisting minister:
> For those who have fallen asleep in the hope of rising again, that they may see God face to face.

> **We pray to the Lord.**
> R. Lord, hear our prayer.

For the mourners

Assisting minister:

For the family and friends of our brother/sister N., that they may be consoled in their grief by the Lord, who wept at the death of his friend Lazarus.

We pray to the Lord.
R. Lord, hear our prayer.

Assisting minister:

For all of us assembled here to worship in faith, that we may be gathered together again in God's kingdom.

We pray to the Lord.
R. Lord, hear our prayer.

The Priest then concludes:

God, our shelter and our strength,
you listen in love to the cry of your people:
hear the prayers we offer for our departed brothers and sisters.
Cleanse them of their sins
and grant them the fullness of redemption.
We ask this through Christ our Lord.
R. Amen.

H3 (OCF, 401-2)

The Priest begins:

My dear friends, let us join with one another in praying to God, not only for our departed brother/sister, but also for the Church, for peace in the world, and for ourselves.

Assisting minister:

That the bishops and priests of the Church, and all who preach the Gospel, may be given the strength to express in action the word they proclaim.

We pray to the Lord.
R. Lord, hear our prayer.

That those in public office may promote justice and peace.

We pray to the Lord.

R. Lord, hear our prayer.

That those who bear the cross of pain
in mind or body may never feel forsaken by God.

We pray to the Lord.
R. Lord, hear our prayer.

That God may deliver the soul of his servant N. from
punishment and from the powers of darkness.

We pray to the Lord.
R. Lord, hear our prayer.

That God in his mercy may blot out all his (her) offenses.

We pray to the Lord.
R. Lord, hear our prayer.

That God may establish him (her) in light and peace.

We pray to the Lord.
R. Lord, hear our prayer.

That God may call him (her) to happiness in the company of
all the saints.

We pray to the Lord.
R. Lord, hear our prayer.

That God may welcome into his glory those of our family and
friends who have departed this life.

We pray to the Lord.
R. Lord, hear our prayer.

That God may give a place in the kingdom of heaven to all the
faithful departed.

We pray to the Lord.
R. Lord, hear our prayer.

The Priest then concludes:
O God,
Creator and Redeemer of all the faithful,
grant to the souls of your departed servants

release from all their sins.
Hear our prayers for those we love
and give them the pardon they have always desired.

We ask this through Christ our Lord.
R. Amen.

H4 (OCF, 401-4)

The Priest begins:
Let us turn to Christ Jesus with confidence and faith in the
power of his cross and resurrection:

Assisting minister:
Risen Lord, pattern of our life for ever:
Lord, have mercy.
R. Lord, have mercy.

Promise and image of what we shall be:
Lord, have mercy.
R. Lord, have mercy.

Son of God who came to destroy sin and death:
Lord, have mercy.
R. Lord, have mercy.

Word of God who delivered us from the fear of death:
Lord, have mercy.
R. Lord, have mercy.

Crucified Lord, forsaken in death, raised in glory:
Lord, have mercy.
R. Lord, have mercy.

Lord Jesus, gentle Shepherd who brings rest to our souls, give
peace to N. for ever:
Lord, have mercy.
R. Lord, have mercy.

Lord Jesus, you bless those who mourn and are in pain. Bless
N.'s family and friends who gather around him (her) today:
Lord, have mercy.
R. Lord, have mercy.

For a Baptized Child

H5   (OCF, 401-5)

The Priest begins:

Jesus is the Son of God and the pattern for our own creation.
His promise is that one day we shall truly be like him. With
our hope founded on that promise, we pray:

Assisting minister:

That God will receive our praise and thanksgiving for the life
of N.:

Let us pray to the Lord.
R. Lord, have mercy.

That God will bring to completion N.'s baptism into Christ:

Let us pray to the Lord.
R. Lord, have mercy.

That God will lead N. from death to life:

Let us pray to the Lord.
R. Lord, have mercy.

That all of us, N.'s family and friends, may be comforted in our
grief:

Let us pray to the Lord.
R. Lord, have mercy.

That God will grant release to those who suffer:

Let us pray to the Lord.
R. Lord, have mercy.

That God will grant peace to all who have died in the faith of
Christ:

Let us pray to the Lord.
R. Lord, have mercy.

That one day we may all share in the banquet of the Lord,
praising God for victory over death:

Let us pray to the Lord.
R. Lord, have mercy.

For a Baptized Child

H6 (OCF, 401-6)

The Priest begins:
> The Lord Jesus is the lover of his people and our only sure
> hope. Let us ask him to deepen our faith and sustain us in this
> dark hour.

Assisting minister:
> You became a little child for our sake, sharing our human life.
>
> To you we pray:
> R. Bless us and keep us, O Lord.

> You grew in wisdom, age, and grace, and learned obedience
> through suffering.
>
> To you we pray:
> R. Bless us and keep us, O Lord.

> You welcomed children, promising them your kingdom.
>
> To you we pray:
> R. Bless us and keep us, O Lord.

> You comforted those who mourned the loss of children and
> friends.
>
> To you we pray:
> R. Bless us and keep us, O Lord.

You took upon yourself the suffering and death of us all.

To you we pray:
R. Bless us and keep us, O Lord.

You promised to raise up those who believe in you just as you
were raised up in glory by the Father.

To you we pray:
R. Bless us and keep us, O Lord.

The Priest then concludes:
Lord God, you entrusted N. to our care
and now you embrace him (her) in your love.
Take N. into your keeping
together with all children who have died.
Comfort us, your sorrowing servants,
who seek to do your will
and to know your saving peace.

We ask this through Christ our Lord.
R. Amen.

For a Child

H7

(OCF, 401-7)

The Priest begins:
Let us pray for N., his (her) family and friends, and for all
God's people.

Assisting minister:
For N., child of God [and heir to the kingdom], that he (she) be
held securely in God's loving embrace now and for all eternity.

We pray to the Lord.
R. Lord, hear our prayer.

For N.'s family, especially his (her) mother and father, [his
(her) brother(s) and sister(s)], that they feel the healing power
of Christ in the midst of their pain and grief.

We pray to the Lord.
R. Lord, hear our prayer.

For N.'s friends, those who played with him (her) and those who cared for him (her), that they may be consoled in their loss and strengthened in their love for one another.
We pray to the Lord.
R. Lord, hear our prayer.

For all parents who grieve over the death of their children, that they may be comforted in the knowledge that their children dwell with God.
We pray to the Lord.
R. Lord, hear our prayer.

For children who have died of hunger and disease, that these little ones be seated close to the Lord at his heavenly table.
We pray to the Lord.
R. Lord, hear our prayer.

For the whole Church, that we prepare worthily for the hour of our death, when God will call us by name to pass from this world to the next.
We pray to the Lord.
R. Lord, hear our prayer.

The Priest then concludes:
Lord God,
you entrusted N. to our care
and now you embrace him (her) in your love.

Take N. into your keeping
together with all children who have died.

Comfort us, your sorrowing servants,
who seek to do your will
and to know your saving peace.

We ask this through Christ our Lord.
R. Amen.

Liturgy of the Eucharist

Preparation of the Altar and Gifts
Prayer over the Offerings
Preface
Eucharistic Prayer
Prayer after Communion

Preparation of the Altar and Gifts

Members of the family or friends of the deceased may bring the offerings of bread and wine to the altar.

Prayer over the Offerings

Outside Easter Time

J1 (RM, Funeral Mass A)

As we humbly present to you
these sacrificial offerings, O Lord,
for the salvation of your servant N.,
we beseech your mercy,
that he (she), who did not doubt your Son
to be a loving Savior,
may find in him a merciful Judge.

Who lives and reigns for ever and ever.
R. Amen.

J2
(RM, Funeral Mass B)

Be near, O Lord, we pray, to your servant N.,
on whose funeral day
we offer you this sacrifice of conciliation,
so that, should any stain of sin have clung to him (her)
or any human fault have affected him (her),
it may, by your loving gift, be forgiven and wiped away.

Through Christ our Lord.
R. Amen.

During Easter Time

J3
(RM, Funeral Mass C)

Look favorably on our offerings, O Lord,
so that your departed servant N.
may be taken up into glory with your Son,
in whose great mystery of love we are all united.

Through Christ our Lord.
R. Amen.

General

J4
(RM, Funeral Mass D)

Almighty and merciful God,
by means of these sacrificial offerings,
wash away, we pray, in the Blood of Christ,
the sins of your departed servant N.,
and purify unceasingly by your merciful forgiveness
those you once cleansed in the waters of Baptism.

Through Christ our Lord.
R. Amen.

For a Baptized Child

J5

(RM, Funeral Mass E)

Sanctify these offerings we bring you, O Lord,
that the parents, who now entrust to you
the child you gave to them,
may come to embrace him (her) with joy in your Kingdom.

Through Christ our Lord.
R. Amen.

J6

Graciously accept this offering, O God,
as a sign of our devotion,
so that, trusting in the designs of your providence,
we may be raised up by your gentle and fatherly care.

Through Christ our Lord.
R. Amen.

For a Child Who Died before Baptism

J7

(RM, Funeral Mass F)

Graciously accept this offering, O God,
as a sign of our devotion,
so that, trusting in the designs of your providence,
we may be raised up by your gentle and fatherly care.

Through Christ our Lord.
R. Amen.

Preface

The preface is the beginning of the Eucharistic Prayer and starts with a liturgical dialogue. Please choose from among the five options presented and record your choice on the selection sheet.

K1   (RM, Masses for the Dead, Preface I)

V. The Lord be with you.
R. And with your spirit.

V. Lift up your hearts.
R. We lift them up to the Lord.

V. Let us give thanks to the Lord our God.
R. It is right and just.

It is truly right and just, our duty and our salvation,
always and everywhere to give you thanks,
Lord, holy Father, almighty and eternal God,
through Christ our Lord.
In him the hope of blessed resurrection has dawned,
that those saddened by the certainty of dying
might be consoled by the promise of immortality to come.
Indeed for your faithful, Lord,
life is changed not ended,
and, when this earthly dwelling turns to dust,
an eternal dwelling is made ready for them in heaven.
And so, with Angels and Archangels,
with Thrones and Dominions,
and with all the hosts and Powers of heaven,
we sing the hymn of your glory,
as without end we acclaim:

Holy, Holy, Holy Lord God of hosts . . .

K2   (RM, Masses for the Dead, Preface II)

V. The Lord be with you.
R. And with your spirit.

V. Lift up your hearts.
R. We lift them up to the Lord.

V. Let us give thanks to the Lord our God.
R. It is right and just.

It is truly right and just, our duty and our salvation,
always and everywhere to give you thanks,
Lord, holy Father, almighty and eternal God,
through Christ our Lord.
For as one alone he accepted death,
so that we might all escape from dying;
as one man he chose to die,
so that in your sight we all might live for ever.
And so, in company with the choirs of Angels,
we praise you, and with joy we proclaim:

Holy, Holy, Holy Lord God of hosts . . .

K3

(RM, Masses for the Dead, Preface III)

V. The Lord be with you.
R. And with your spirit.

V. Lift up your hearts.
R. We lift them up to the Lord.

V. Let us give thanks to the Lord our God.
R. It is right and just.

It is truly right and just, our duty and our salvation,
always and everywhere to give you thanks,
Lord, holy Father, almighty and eternal God,
through Christ our Lord.
For he is the salvation of the world,
the life of the human race,
the resurrection of the dead.
Through him the host of Angels adores your majesty
and rejoices in your presence for ever.
May our voices, we pray, join with theirs
in one chorus of exultant praise, as we acclaim:

Holy, Holy, Holy Lord God of hosts . . .

K4   (RM, Masses for the Dead, Preface IV)

V. The Lord be with you.
R. And with your spirit.

V. Lift up your hearts.
R. We lift them up to the Lord.

V. Let us give thanks to the Lord our God.
R. It is right and just.

It is truly right and just, our duty and our salvation,
always and everywhere to give you thanks,
Lord, holy Father, almighty and eternal God.
For it is at your summons that we come to birth,
by your will that we are governed,
and at your command that we return,
on account of sin,
to that earth from which we came.
And when you give the sign,
we who have been redeemed by the Death of your Son,
shall be raised up to the glory of his Resurrection.
And so, with the company of Angels and Saints,
we sing the hymn of your praise,
as without end we acclaim:

Holy, Holy, Holy Lord God of hosts . . .

K5   (RM, Masses for the Dead, Preface V)

V. The Lord be with you.
R. And with your spirit.

V. Lift up your hearts.
R. We lift them up to the Lord.

V. Let us give thanks to the Lord our God.
R. It is right and just.

It is truly right and just, our duty and our salvation,
always and everywhere to give you thanks,

Lord, holy Father, almighty and eternal God.
For even though by our own fault we perish,
yet by your compassion and your grace,
when seized by death according to our sins,
we are redeemed through Christ's great victory,
and with him called back into life.
And so, with the Powers of heaven,
we worship you constantly on earth,
and before your majesty
without end we acclaim:

Holy, Holy, Holy Lord God of hosts . . .

Eucharistic Prayer

*Eucharistic Prayers II and III are especially appropriate for use at the Funeral
Mass, because they provide special texts of intercession for the dead. You may
choose one of the options that follows and record it on the selection sheet.*

From Eucharistic Prayer II:

L1 (RM, 105)

Remember your servant N.,
whom you have called (today)
from this world to yourself.
Grant that he (she) who was united with your Son in a death
like his,
may also be one with him in his Resurrection.

From Eucharistic Prayer III:

L2   (RM, 115)

> Remember your servant N.
> whom you have called (today)
> from this world to yourself.
> Grant that he (she) who was united with your Son in a death
>   like his,
> may also be one with him in his Resurrection,
> when from the earth
> he will raise up in the flesh those who have died,
> and transform our lowly body
> after the pattern of his own glorious body.
> To our departed brothers and sisters, too,
> and to all who were pleasing to you
> at their passing from this life,
> give kind admittance to your kingdom.
> There we hope to enjoy for ever the fullness of your glory,
> when you will wipe away every tear from our eyes.
> For seeing you, our God, as you are,
> we shall be like you for all the ages
> and praise you without end,
> through Christ our Lord,
> through whom you bestow on the world all that is good.

Prayer after Communion

After the distribution of Holy Communion is finished, there is a brief period of silent prayer in which the assembled community offers thanksgiving to God. Then the Priest prays aloud one of the following prayers. Please record your choice on your selection sheet.

Outside Easter Time   (RM, Funeral Mass A, B)

N1

> Lord God, whose Son left us,
> in the Sacrament of his Body,
> food for the journey,

mercifully grant that, strengthened by it,
our brother (sister) N. may come
to the eternal table of Christ.

Who lives and reigns for ever and ever.
R. Amen.

N2

Grant, we pray, almighty God,
that your servant N.,
who (today) has journeyed from this world,
may by this sacrifice be cleansed and freed from sin
and so receive the everlasting joys of the resurrection.

Through Christ our Lord.
R. Amen.

During the Easter Season (RM, Funeral Mass C)

N3

Grant, we pray, O Lord, that your servant N.,
for whom we have celebrated this paschal Sacrament,
may pass over to a dwelling place of light and peace.

Through Christ our Lord.
R. Amen.

General (RM, Funeral Mass D)

N4

Having received the Sacrament of your Only Begotten Son,
who was sacrificed for us and rose in glory,
we humbly implore you, O Lord,
for your departed servant N.,
that, cleansed by the paschal mysteries,
he (she) may glory in the gift of the resurrection to come.

Through Christ our Lord.
R. Amen.

For a Baptized Child

N5

Having received the Communion
of your Son's Body and Blood, O Lord,
we ask you faithfully
to comfort amid the sorrows of this life
those whom you have graciously nourished
by these sacred mysteries,
so as to strengthen their hope of life eternal.

Through Christ our Lord.
R. Amen.

N6

Nourished by your divine gifts,
we pray, O Lord,
that, just as you have given this little child
a place at the table in your heavenly Kingdom,
we, too, may find a place there.

Through Christ our Lord.
R. Amen.

For a Child Who Died before Baptism

N7

Having received the Communion
of your Son's Body and Blood, O Lord,
we ask you faithfully
to comfort amid the sorrows of this life
those whom you have graciously nourished
by these sacred mysteries,
so as to strengthen their hope of life eternal.

Through Christ our Lord.
R. Amen.

Final Commendation

Remarks of Remembrance
Invitation to Prayer
Silence
Signs of Farewell
Song of Farewell
Prayer of Commendation

Remarks of Remembrance

Following the prayer after communion a member or a friend of the family may speak in remembrance of the deceased.

Invitation to Prayer

The Priest faces the people and invites them to pray using these or similar words:

O1
(OCF, 171-A)

Before we go our separate ways, let us take leave of our brother/ sister. May our farewell express our affection for him (her); may it ease our sadness and strengthen our hope. One day we shall joyfully greet him (her) again when the love of Christ, which conquers all things, destroys even death itself.

02

(OCF, 171-B)

Trusting in God, we have prayed together for N. and now we come to the last farewell. There is sadness in parting, but we take comfort in the hope that one day we shall see N. again and enjoy his (her) friendship. Although this congregation will disperse in sorrow, the mercy of God will gather us together again in the joy of his kingdom. Therefore let us console one another in the faith of Jesus Christ.

03

(OCF, 402-1)

With faith in Jesus Christ, we must reverently bury the body of our brother/sister.

Let us pray with confidence to God, in whose sight all creation lives, that he will raise up in holiness and power the mortal body of our brother/sister and command his (her) soul to be numbered among the blessed.

May God grant him (her) a merciful judgment, deliverance from death, and pardon of sin. May Christ the Good Shepherd carry him (her) home to be at peace with the Father. May he (she) rejoice for ever in the presence of the eternal King and in the company of all the saints.

04

(OCF, 402-2)

Our brother/sister N. has fallen asleep in Christ. Confident in our hope of eternal life, let us commend him (her) to the loving mercy of our Father and let our prayers go with him (her). He (she) was adopted as God's son/daughter in baptism and was nourished at the table of the Lord; may he (she) now inherit the promise of eternal life and take his (her) place at the table of God's children in heaven.

Let us pray also on our own behalf, that we who now mourn and are saddened may one day go forth with our brother/sister to meet the Lord of life when he appears in glory.

O5 (OCF, 402-3)

Because God has chosen to call our brother/sister N.
from this life to himself,
we commit his (her) body to the earth,
for we are dust and unto dust we shall return.
But the Lord Jesus Christ will change our mortal bodies to be
like his in glory,
for he is risen, the firstborn from the dead.
So let us commend our brother/sister to the Lord,
that the Lord may embrace him (her) in peace
and raise up his (her) body on the last day.

O6 (OCF, 402-4)

Before we go our separate ways, let us take leave of our
brother/sister. May our farewell express our affection for him
(her); may it ease our sadness and strengthen our hope. One
day we shall joyfully greet him (her) again when the love of
Christ, which conquers all things, destroys even death itself.

Silence (OCF, 172)

All pray in silence.

Signs of Farewell (OCF, 173)

*[The coffin may now be sprinkled with holy water and incensed, or this may
take place during or after the song of farewell. If the body was sprinkled with
holy water during the rite of reception at the beginning of the funeral liturgy, the
sprinkling is ordinarily omitted in the rite of final commendation.]*

Song of Farewell (OCF, 174)

*The song of farewell is sung. The texts below or other similar ones may be used,
or another song may be sung.*

P1 (OCF, 174)

Saints of God, come to his (her) aid!
Hasten to meet him (her), angels of the Lord!

R. **Receive his (her) soul and present him (her) to God the Most
High.**

May Christ, who called you, take you to himself;
may angels lead you to the bosom of Abraham.

R. **Receive his (her) soul and present him (her) to God the Most
High.**

Eternal rest grant unto him (her), O Lord,
and let perpetual light shine upon him (her).

R. **Receive his (her) soul and present him (her) to God the Most
High.**

P2 (OCF, 403-2)

Lord our God, receive your servant, for whom you shed your
blood.

R. **Remember, Lord, that we are dust: like grass, like a flower
of the field.**

Merciful Lord, I tremble before you, ashamed of the things I have
done.

R. **Remember, Lord, that we are dust: like grass, like a flower
of the field.**

P3 (OCF, 403-3)

You knew me, Lord, before I was born.
You shaped me into your image and likeness.

R. **I breathe forth my spirit to you, my Creator.**

Merciful Lord, I tremble before you:
I am ashamed of the things I have done;
do not condemn me when you come in judgment.

R. **I breathe forth my spirit to you, my Creator.**

P4 (OCF, 403-4)

I know that my Redeemer lives:
on the last day I shall rise again.

R. And in my flesh I shall see God.
or:
R. On the last day I shall rise again.

I shall see him myself, face to face;
and my own eyes shall behold my Savior.

R. And in my flesh I shall see God.
or:
R. On the last day I shall rise again.

Within my heart this hope I cherish:
that in my flesh I shall see God.

R. And in my flesh I shall see God.
or:
R. On the last day I shall rise again.

P5 (OCF, 403-5)

I know that my Redeemer lives,
And on that final day of days,
His voice shall bid me rise again:
Unending joy, unceasing praise!
This hope I cherish in my heart:
To stand on earth, my flesh restored,
And, not a stranger but a friend,
Behold my Savior and my Lord.

P6   (OCF, 403-6)

Lazarus you raised, O Lord, from the decay of the tomb.

R. **Grant your servant rest, a haven of pardon and peace.**

Eternal rest, O Lord,
and your perpetual light.

R. **Grant your servant rest, a haven of pardon and peace.**

P7   (OCF, 403-7)

You shattered the gates of bronze
and preached to the spirits in prison.

R. **Deliver me, Lord, from the streets of darkness.**

A light and a revelation
to those confined in darkness.

R. **Deliver me, Lord, from the streets of darkness.**

"Redeemer, you have come,"
they cried, the prisoners of silence.

R. **Deliver me, Lord, from the streets of darkness.**

Eternal rest, O Lord,
and your perpetual light.

R. **Deliver me, Lord, from the streets of darkness.**

Prayer of Commendation

The Priest says one of the following prayers:

Q1 (OCF, 175-A)

Into your hands, Father of mercies,
we commend our brother/sister N.
in the sure and certain hope
that, together with all who have died in Christ,
he (she) will rise with him on the last day.
[We give you thanks for the blessings
which you bestowed upon N. in this life:
they are signs to us of your goodness
and of our fellowship with the saints in Christ.]
Merciful Lord,
turn toward us and listen to our prayers:
open the gates of paradise to your servant
and help us who remain
to comfort one another with assurances of faith,
until we all meet in Christ
and are with you and with our brother/sister for ever.

We ask this through Christ our Lord.
R. Amen.

Q2 (OCF, 175-B)

To you, O Lord, we commend the soul of N. your servant;
in the sight of this world he (she) is now dead;
in your sight may he (she) live for ever.
Forgive whatever sins he (she) committed through human
weakness
and in your goodness grant him (her) everlasting peace.

We ask this through Christ our Lord.
R. Amen.

A Baptized Person

Q3
(OCF, 404-1)

Into your hands, Father of mercies,
we commend our brother/sister N.
in the sure and certain hope
that, together with all who have died in Christ,
he (she) will rise with him on the last day.
[We give you thanks for the blessings
which you bestowed upon N. in this life:
they are signs to us of your goodness
and of our fellowship with the saints in Christ.]
Merciful Lord,
turn toward us and listen to our prayers:
open the gates of paradise to your servant
and help us who remain
to comfort one another with assurances of faith,
until we all meet in Christ
and are with you and with our brother/sister for ever.

We ask this through Christ our Lord.
R. Amen.

A Baptized Child

Q4
(OCF, 404-2)

Lord Jesus,
like a shepherd who gathers the lambs
to protect them from all harm,
you led N. to the waters of baptism
and shielded him (her) in innocence.
Now carry this little one
on the path to your kingdom of light
where he (she) will find happiness
and every tear will be wiped away.

To you be glory, now and for ever.
R. Amen.

Q5

Into your gentle keeping, O Lord,
we commend this child [N.].
Though our hearts are troubled,
we hope in your loving kindness.
By the sign of the cross
he (she) was claimed for Christ,
and in the waters of baptism
he (she) died with Christ to live in him for ever.
May the angels, our guardians,
lead N. now to paradise
where your saints will welcome him (her)
and every tear will be wiped away.
There we shall join in songs of praise for ever.

We ask this through Christ our Lord.
R. Amen.

Procession to the Place of Committal

(OCF, 176)

The deacon or Priest says:
In peace let us take our brother/sister to his (her) place of rest.

If a symbol of the Christian life has been placed on the coffin, it should be removed at this time. The pall may be removed before the procession begins or at the entrance to the church. The Priest and assisting ministers precede the coffin while the family and mourners follow. A suitable song is sung during the procession to the entrance of the church.

Appendix: Cremation

The Catholic Church holds the bodies of its deceased members in the highest regard. Great reverence is due the human body in all stages, from conception through death and on to its final resting place. We have traditionally buried our dead in the ground or in tombs as Christ was buried. In earlier centuries, the practice was upheld over the pagan practice of cremation in certain places.

Burial continues to be the Church's preference and our funeral rites for the most part assume the presence of the body. While we no longer have need to distinguish ourselves from people of other faiths or no faith, the presence of the body during the funeral rites heightens our focus on the hope of the resurrection and our being reunited with our loved one in the world to come.

The Church permits cremation so long as it is not chosen because of a denial of belief in the resurrection or denial of any other Catholic teaching. Certainly cremation is becoming more and more common, especially in places where burial ground is scarce, where environmental stewardship suggests it is a prudent choice, or where financial concerns warrant it. When cremation is chosen, the *Order of Christian Funerals* urges that the body be present in church for the funeral when at all possible, with cremation taking place afterward. This helps the loved ones of the deceased to make their final farewell within the gathered community of faith, supported by the prayers, blessings, and ceremonies of the Church's liturgy.

When it is not possible or practical to have the body present for the funeral, liturgical norms allow the Funeral Mass to be celebrated in the presence of the cremated remains, so long as the local ordinary (bishop in charge of a diocese) has granted this permission. Whether cremation occurs prior to or following the funeral, cremated remains are to be treated with the same respect as is given to the human body. They should be buried in a grave or entombed in a mausoleum or columbarium. The Church does not permit the scattering of cremated remains nor the keeping of these in homes.

The funeral liturgy in the presence of cremated remains varies only slightly from that of a funeral where the body is present. The priest assisting you in preparing the funeral will help you understand just how the liturgy will unfold.

To learn more about cremation in the Catholic Church, consider reading the short document *Reflections on the Body, Cremation, and Catholic Funeral Rites* published in 1997 by the United States Conference of Catholic Bishops.

Msgr. Joseph M. Champlin served in sacramental ministry as resident priest at Our Lady of Good Counsel in Warners, New York. He was the former rector of the Cathedral of the Immaculate Conception in his home Diocese of Syracuse. A prolific writer on a variety of pastoral care and spirituality concerns, he was also a regular featured guest on *Seize the Day with Gus Lloyd*, a show that airs on Sirius Radio channel 159. Champlin had traveled more than two million miles lecturing in the United States and abroad. Among his more than fifty books are: *Slow Down* and *Take Five* (Sorin Books), *Should We Marry?*, *From the Heart*, *Together for Life*®, and *Through Death to Life* (Ave Maria Press). Joseph Champlin died in January 2008.

Selection Sheet

Funeral Mass for _____

Date _____ Time _____

Presiding Priest _____

Church _____

Introductory Rites

Greeting: pages 1–2   No. _____

    Placing of the Pall: page 2

    ____ Priest   ____ Family or ____ Friend

    Placing of Christian Symbols: page 3

    ____ Priest   ____ Family or ____ Friend

Collect: pages 3–23   No. _____

Liturgy of the Word

Reading I: pages 26–34   No. _____

Read by: _____

Responsorial Psalm: pages 35–44   No. _____

Read or Sung by: _____

Reading II: pages 45–55   No. _____

Read by: _____

Alleluia Verse and Verse Before the Gospel: pages 56–58 No. _____

Gospel Reading: pages 58–78   No. _____

General Intercessions: pages 79–89   No. _____

Read by: _____

Liturgy of the Eucharist

Presentation of the Gifts by: _____

Prayer over the Gifts: pages 91–93   No. _____

Preface: pages 93–97   No. _____

Eucharistic Prayer: II or III pages 97–98   No. _____

Prayer after Communion: pages 98–100   No. _____

Final Commendation

Remarks of Remembrance by: _____

Invitation to Prayer: pages 101–103   No. _____

Song of Farewell: pages 104–106   No. _____

Prayer of Commendation: pages 107–109   No. _____